THE PENGUIN

EDITED BY E.

L 8

VIRGIL
THE PASTORAL POEMS

THE TEXT OF THE ECLOGUES
WITH A TRANSLATION

BY E. V. RIEU

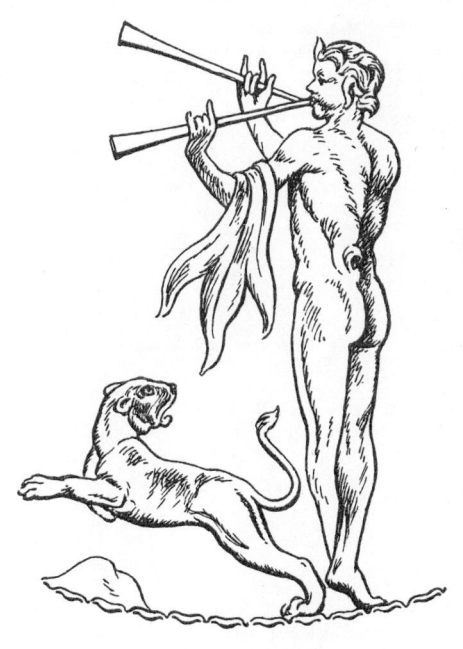

PENGUIN BOOKS
BALTIMORE · MARYLAND

Penguin Books Ltd, Harmondsworth, Middlesex
U.S.A.: Penguin Books Inc., 3300 Clipper Mill Road, Baltimore 11, Md
AUSTRALIA: Penguin Books Pty Ltd, 762 Whitehorse Road,
Mitcham, Victoria

—

THIS TRANSLATION,
SPECIALLY MADE FOR PENGUIN BOOKS LTD,
WAS FIRST PUBLISHED IN 1949
REPRINTED IN 1953
REPRINTED, WITH LATIN TEXT, 1954, 1961

—

Made and printed in Great Britain
by Hunt, Barnard & Co, Ltd,
Aylesbury

CONTENTS

INTRODUCTION

I

THE aim of this translation of Virgil's Pastoral Poems, the *Eclogues* (or *Select Pieces*), as they are usually called, is to introduce new readers to the unknown delights of Latin poetry. These poems were the first that Virgil published in book form. They have a strong individuality of their own, which has remained fresh and unimpaired through twenty centuries of false and true appreciation. Yet, like all the most significant works of art, they are largely representative of their period too. No happier entry could be found to the golden age of Roman letters.

Of the man who wrote them, apart from what he himself reveals, we know only too little – more than of Homer or Shakespeare, rather less than of Chaucer, much less than of Milton. This is so true that controversial statements cannot be excluded even from the briefest outline of his life.

Publius Vergilius Maro (to give him his full Latin name and spell it correctly) was born in 70 B.C. at the village of Andes, which lay not very far, though its exact location is disputed, from the small town of Mantua, in that part of Northern Italy which was called Cisalpine Gaul. His people may be described as yeoman stock. His father, who combined farming with bee-keeping on a commercial scale, had the resources and the foresight to give him a sound schooling, at Cremona first, and later at Milan. He was even prosperous enough to send his son to Rome, at the age of seventeen, to complete his education and prepare for a career. Virgil's university training, as we should now call it, began with a course of rhetoric. But the elder Virgil had misjudged the shy and sensitive genius of his son, who discovered, after a maiden speech in court, that he was not cut out for success in politics or at the bar. After this false start, Virgil turned to philosophy, with an enthusiasm that he has himself described for us in a charming little poem, and sat, for some years, it seems, at the feet of the Epicurean lecturer, Siro, in Naples. Siro was popular with the rich and ambitious youth of the day, and it was at this time that Virgil formed those friendships with the future leaders of political and intellectual life that we hear of in the *Eclogues*. He had already tried his hand at verse – we have several of his early efforts[1] – but he had not found himself yet; and there is good reason for believing that the impulse which produced the *Eclogues* was the outcome of this prolonged period of philosophic study and of the literary contacts it afforded.

In embracing philosophy, Virgil had begged the Muse of poetry not to abandon him altogether, but to make her visits 'rare and seemly'. She took him at his word. He was a slow worker, and years passed before the *Eclogues* took shape. In fact, though written at odd times in his third decade, the collection was not published till Virgil was thirty-one, in the year 39 B.C., by which time his friend Cornelius Gallus, a younger member of the literary coterie I

1. Many, at any rate, of the short poems in the collection entitled *Catalepton* are now considered to be genuine by competent authorities.

have referred to, already had several well-established volumes of verse to his credit. There is something very characteristic of Virgil's diffident and late-maturing genius in this delay. Moreover, he was an awkward and shy, though attractive, young man. One can almost believe that he would not have published at all, had the friends who already knew his poems not forced him to do so, and that no rising poet was ever so embarrassed by the popular success that his work achieved. For it seems to have taken Rome by storm. The *Eclogues* were even recited or sung in the theatre – by no means a regular by-product, in those days, of publication in book form – and their author received such acclamations as were generally reserved for the ruler of the Roman world.

His reputation was now established. He became, if not the 'court poet' of the early Empire (for he preserved his integrity to the very end), the poet most esteemed at court. Octavian's minister, Maecenas, encouraged him in the production of his next work, the *Georgics*, over which he toiled for seven years, living for the most part in Southern Italy; and, when this was done, Octavian himself fostered and cherished in all the slow stages of its growth the still greater work which occupied his last decade. He died (19 B.C.) in his fifty-first year, and the *Aeneid*, which he had ordered to be burnt, was published in its unfinished form by his literary executors, at the Emperor's command.

II

Before returning to the *Eclogues* it will be well to glance at the history of Virgil's day, although the direct references which he makes to contemporary events are scarcely more numerous than those which Jane Austen makes in her novels to the Napoleonic Wars. When he first saw the reeds of Mincius and the foot-hills of the Alps, the aristocratic regime in Italy, which we call the Republic, was already tottering to its fall, and, during the whole of his second decade, Julius Caesar, who was destined to destroy it, was engaged on those campaigns in Gaul which enabled him eventually to cross the Rubicon with a devoted force and make his decisive march on Rome (49 B.C.). The civil wars that followed his seizure of power were renewed rather than terminated by his assassination five years later, when Virgil was twenty-six, and it took Octavian, the young grandnephew whom Julius had adopted as his son and successor, thirteen years to overcome, first his father's murderers, and then his own associate and rival, Antony. The battle of Actium (31 B.C.) settled Antony's fate, and brought peace, with despotism, to the Roman world. Octavian finally established himself as 'Princeps' in 27 B.C., took the title of Augustus, and under that name is known to us as the first emperor of Rome.

To these catastrophic events, Virgil (though there is a story that in spite of his poor health he fought in one campaign), reacted rather as a poet and a thinker than as a politician or a partisan. It is true that he admired Julius Caesar – as a boy he may well have

Spenser, Milton, Pope, Tennyson – when they drank at their source, found other qualities in the *Eclogues* than this. Yet it must be admitted that in the long run it was the tendency of imitators to emphasize the apparent artificiality of the original. In the 19th century it was possible for serious critics to speak of the *Eclogues* as though they were as spurious as the Watteau shepherdesses whose distant ancestors they are. John Conington, for instance, stressing and misinterpreting Virgil's debt to the Greek pastoral poet Theocritus, grants him some felicity of style, but condemns his whole work as 'unreal', as 'palpable and avowed imitation', and even as a 'corruption' of literature. And though, among Conington's contemporaries, the *Eclogues* found other and less censorious devotees, I suspect that with many of them it was their prettiness rather than their depth that counted. It was left to the 20th-century critics to rediscover their excellence, and they did their work almost too well, for the diversity of their findings, though a tribute to Virgil's many-sided genius, is perplexing. Tenney Frank, in his important biography of the poet, cleared away many ancient misinterpretations on allegorical lines, brought Virgil and his times to life, and presented the *Eclogues* as a sincere and sympathetic study of the pastoral life of the day. E. K. Rand, in an equally illuminating study, *The Magical Art of Virgil*, showed us the poet working his way through the pastoral to the epic form, and brought out the element of hero-worship that figures in the work. Meanwhile J. S. Phillimore, in his *Pastoral and Allegory*, had put new life into the allegorical view of the poems, emphasizing Virgil's importance in the circle of young writers within which he worked, and leaving us to regard each Eclogue as bearing direct reference to the lost work of some other member of this coterie. Finally, the most recent translator of Virgil makes a new and surprising departure down the old cul-de-sac by dismissing the *Eclogues* as the immature and artificial experiments of a youthful poet.

The poems have many facets, and there is truth in nearly all these views – even in Conington's. Virgil did present the Greek idyl to the Latin world: he was the Roman Theocritus. Yet at the same time his pastoral sketches were not out-of-date nor purely fanciful: they were closely related to the peasants' experiences in a time of strife and disorder. Again, still anchoring himself to external realities, he did seize occasions to praise the great men of the day. And those scholars too are right who suggest that, if we had the poems of Gallus and Virgil's other friends in our hands, we should find a wealth of subtle allusion, even of parody, in his work.

But I am left with the feeling that Virgil not only could, but did, achieve all these aims, and something else as well; that they conditioned the form his writing took, but did not inspire it. Behind them all, I detect an overriding poetic impulse, which persists through the diversity of all ten pieces, justified Virgil in making one book of them, accounts for their early success, and – still more important from our point of view – explains the fact that 20th-century people who know little of the politics and literature of Virgil's times, and care less, can still succumb to their enchantment.

If then I must embark on my own interpretation, I should say that what inspired and unifies the *Eclogues* is a poet's perception of certain realities that underlie our relation to the world around us. It was in his Arcady, the pastoral world of his memories and of his fancy, that Virgil found the window which gave him this vision of the truth, and sensed the spirit that pulsates in everything that is, and makes a harmony of man, tree, beast, and rock. Nature is fundamentally at one with man, though towns and politics and war make him a refugee from her and from the truth. It is the shepherd and his sheep that are her nurslings and her confidants. It is they who comprehend, when the 'woods on Maenalus make music and the pine-trees speak'. Virgil had listened with them as a boy, and he remembers and reports what he had heard and seen – a world where everything is quick with understanding, where 'the rocks burst into song and the plantations speak'; where brooks are checked and lynxes overcome by the music of the reeds aroused from their native indolence by Pan; where the pipe itself instructs the player; where the tamarisk sheds tears for the unhappy lover, and sympathetic sheep stand round him in their grief, while the truant Nymphs who fail to rally to his side are chidden for remissness in their task.

It is easy to dismiss these personifications and pathetic fallacies as the pretty conceits that a Roman poet took over from the teeming world of Greek fancy. But I think it would be wrong. It is at such points that Virgil adds significance to beauty, contacts reality most closely, and expresses his vision and his very self most clearly. It is here that he is most tender and most playful. He invites us to enjoy these touches, not as meretricious adornments, but because they are openings on an unseen and delightful world. The truth he saw is not only a solemn awe-compelling thing, but something that can pierce the trees and rocks with ecstasy, and also make a poet smile. It is an outlook on the world which more than one modern philosophy might not repudiate, even if it failed to recognize the idiom in which Virgil spoke.

I submit then that, through all their diversity and the multitude of subordinate meanings that are rightly found in them, the *Eclogues* are symphonic variations on this elusive theme. Wordsworth had comparable intuitions, which he reports more fully and in other terms. Housman too, when he walked by Onny, Teme, and Clun, saw an Arcady of his own, very different from Virgil's, and with sterner laws in it and sadder men. Virgil himself, when he wrote the *Georgics* in his middle years, developed a different, though parallel, interpretation of man's place in nature. But the *Georgics* are another story. All I have done here is to express sincerely, if inadequately, what one of its lovers finds in Virgil's earliest work.

IV

But the analysis of poetry is apt to defeat its own purpose, and the reader may well ask why, having already given him hints of what I hope he may find in the poems themselves, I should have thought it necessary to comment on them in the series of ten Essays that I have added to this book. Let me tell him at once that, though I could not resist the temptation of writing these, he is under no obligation to read them. If he does so, in spite of this reprieve, he will find that I have attempted, not further explanations of the spirit of the *Eclogues*, but some discussion of the *form* that spirit took, with comments on points of interest in their setting and their history, and a little more information about Virgil's life and times – in fact a not too serious introduction into the fascinating field of Virgilian studies. Any scholar who may happen to pick up this book will readily acquit me of having made anything like a thorough analysis of the difficulties involved. Indeed he is more likely to feel that I have been too light-hearted. But I maintain that we have Virgil's own authority not to take him with too great solemnity. He speaks of his book as a prank he had allowed himself in the audacity of youth. Besides, there are many points in the long history of Virgilian scholarship where it is impossible to restrain a smile.

Some of my indebtedness to previous students I have already implied. The remainder will become even more apparent in the Essays. I will confine myself here to a word on the earliest and perhaps the greatest of them all, the 4th-century scholar, or scholars, whose multiple personality I refer to for the sake of convenience under the single name of Servius. Servius may find more allegories in Virgil than we care to endorse, but he is right in his estimate of the varieties of meaning that are to be sought in his words. He is learned, acute, and full of good things. He knows his Virgil inside out, and if I sometimes venture to make fun of him, it is with the uneasy feeling that the last laugh may rest with him.

In order to avoid footnotes to the poems, I have discussed in the Essays a few points on which the modern reader may be glad of enlightenment. Others, and in particular the unfamiliar names from ancient geography and Greek legend, I have dealt with by devoting a few words to each in a Glossary at the end of the book. Reference to that index is no more essential to the enjoyment of the *Eclogues* than is a reading of the Essays.

Of the translation itself I will only say that it might well have been less like Virgil if I had laboured to render the music of his hexameters in some traditional form of English verse. I have seen no attempt of the kind that has not lost more than it has gained by squeezing Virgil into a mould of alien design.

For many an incisive comment and shrewd suggestion made when this book was in the typescript stage, I am deeply indebted to that seasoned Virgilian scholar, Mr W. F. Jackson Knight. He is not to be held responsible for anything I finally wrote, but without his generous help the work would have been far more faulty than it is. I should be glad to think that the zeal he devoted to *The Pastoral Poems* may stimulate him to produce that new edition of the *Eclogues* which is so much needed today.

The drawing on the title-page is from the Roman salver, called the Neptune Plate, which was recently discovered at Mildenhall and is now displayed in the British Museum. Though the instrument which the young man is playing is not, I think, one of those referred to by Virgil, the artist might also have had the Eighth Eclogue in mind. The picture of Pan on the cover is also taken from the Neptune Plate.

E. V. R.

Highgate, February 1947

For the benefit of students and the entertainment of those who have not quite forgotten their Latin, the text of the *Eclogues* was added to the book in the third impression.

E. V. R.

I

THE DISPOSSESSED

Meliboeus
Tityrus

I

TITYRE, tu patulae recubans sub tegmine fagi
silvestrem tenui musam meditaris avena:
nos patriae fines et dulcia linquimus arva;
nos patriam fugimus: tu, Tityre, lentus in umbra
5 formosam resonare doces Amaryllida silvas.

TITYRUS

O Meliboee, deus nobis haec otia fecit.
namque erit ille mihi semper deus, illius aram
saepe tener nostris ab ovilibus imbuet agnus.
ille meas errare boves, ut cernis, et ipsum
10 ludere quae vellem calamo permisit agresti.

MELIBOEUS

Non equidem invideo; miror magis: undique totis
usque adeo turbatur agris. en, ipse capellas
protinus aeger ago; hanc etiam vix, Tityre, duco.
hic inter densas corylos modo namque gemellos,
15 spem gregis, ah, silice in nuda conixa reliquit.
saepe malum hoc nobis, si mens non laeva fuisset,
de caelo tactas memini praedicere quercus.
sed tamen, iste deus qui sit, da, Tityre, nobis.

TITYRUS

Urbem, quam dicunt Romam, Meliboee, putavi
20 stultus ego huic nostrae similem, quo saepe solemus
pastores ovium teneros depellere fetus.

THE DISPOSSESSED

Meliboeus. Tityrus, while you lie there at ease under the awning of a spreading beech and practise country songs on a light shepherd's pipe, <u>I have to bid good-bye to the home fields and the ploughlands that I love.</u> Exile for me, Tityrus – and you lie sprawling in the shade, teaching the woods to echo back the charms of Amaryllis.

Tityrus. <u>Ah Meliboeus, the man to whom I owe</u> 6 <u>this happy leisure is a god.</u> Yes, I shall always treat him as a god. He shall have an altar, and I will often stain it with the blood of a young lamb from my fold. See for yourself. He gave the word – and my cattle browse at large, while I myself can play the tunes I fancy on my rustic flute.

Meliboeus. Don't think that I am jealous. *My* only 11 feeling is amazement – with every farm in the whole countryside in such a state of chaos. Look at myself, unfit for the road, yet forced to drive my goats on this unending trek. See, Tityrus, I can hardly drag this one along. Just now, in the hazel thicket here, she bore two kids – I had been counting on them – and had to leave the poor things on the naked flints. Ah, if I had not been so blind, I might have known 16 that we were in for this disaster. Often enough I had been warned by Heaven, when lightning struck the oaks.

But tell me, Tityrus, who is this god of yours?

Tityrus. I was a simpleton, Meliboeus. I used to 19 think that the city they call Rome was like our market-town, where we shepherds are accustomed to drive down our new-weaned lambs. Arguing from what I

sic canibus catulos similes, sic matribus haedos
noram, sic parvis componere magna solebam.
verum haec tantum alias inter caput extulit urbes,
25 quantum lenta solent inter viburna cupressi.

MELIBOEUS

Et quae tanta fuit Romam tibi causa videndi?

TITYRUS

Libertas, quae sera tamen respexit inertem,
candidior postquam tondenti barba cadebat,
respexit tamen et longo post tempore venit,
30 postquam nos Amaryllis habet, Galatea reliquit.
namque, fatebor enim, dum me Galatea tenebat,
nec spes libertatis erat, nec cura peculi.
quamvis multa meis exiret victima saeptis,
pinguis et ingratae premeretur caseus urbi,
35 non umquam gravis aere domum mihi dextra redibat.

MELIBOEUS

Mirabar, quid maesta deos, Amarylli, vocares,
cui pendere sua patereris in arbore poma:
Tityrus hinc aberat. ipsae te, Tityre, pinus,
ipsi te fontes, ipsa haec arbusta vocabant.

TITYRUS

40 Quid facerem? neque servitio me exire licebat
nec tam praesentes alibi cognoscere divos.
hic illum vidi iuvenem, Meliboee, quotannis
bis senos cui nostra dies altaria fumant.
hic mihi responsum primus dedit ille petenti:
45 'pascite, ut ante, boves, pueri; submittite tauros.'

knew, from a dog's likeness to a puppy and a goat's to her kids, I measured big by little things. But I soon saw that Rome stands out above all other cities as the cypress soars above the drooping undergrowth.

Meliboeus. And what was the urgent business that took you to Rome?

Tityrus. The call of liberty. I had been lazy; and freedom beckoned to me late – not till the hairs that fell as I clipped my beard began to show a touch of grey. However, the call did come; and after those long years I answered it, when Galatea had thrown me over and Amaryllis had my heart. For I confess that in Galatea's day I entertained no hope of getting free nor cared to save my pence. It made no odds how often a lamb from my fold was chosen for sacrifice, nor what rich cheeses pressed in my dairy went to the thankless town: I never came home with a pocketful of coin.

Meliboeus. Ah, Amaryllis, now I know why you were putting up such wistful prayers and for whose sake you left the apples hanging on the trees! Tityrus had gone. Why, Tityrus, the very pines and springs, the very vineyards here, have sighed for you.

Tityrus. What was a man to do? There was nowhere else than Rome where I could bring my serfdom to an end or find a god so able to protect me. It was there, Meliboeus, that I saw the young man for whom my altar is going to smoke on twelve days in the year. There too that I had from him the first kind answer to my suit. 'Lads,' he said, 'let your cattle graze, as you have always done, and put your bulls to stud.'

MELIBOEUS

Fortunate senex, ergo tua rura manebunt.
et tibi magna satis, quamvis lapis omnia nudus
limosoque palus obducat pascua iunco.
non insueta graves temptabunt pabula fetas,
50 nec mala vicini pecoris contagia laedent.
fortunate senex, hinc inter flumina nota
et fontes sacros frigus captabis opacum.
hinc tibi, quae semper, vicino ab limite saepes
Hyblaeis apibus florem depasta salicti
55 saepe levi somnum suadebit inire susurro;
hinc alta sub rupe canet frondator ad auras:
nec tamen interea raucae, tua cura, palumbes,
nec gemere aëria cessabit turtur ab ulmo.

TITYRUS

Ante leves ergo pascentur in aethere cervi,
60 et freta destituent nudos in litore pisces,
ante pererratis amborum finibus exsul
aut Ararim Parthus bibet aut Germania Tigrim,
quam nostro illius labatur pectore voltus.

MELIBOEUS

At nos hinc alii sitientes ibimus Afros,
65 pars Scythiam et rapidum Cretae veniemus Oaxen
et penitus toto divisos orbe Britannos.
en umquam patrios longo post tempore fines,
pauperis et tuguri congestum caespite culmen

Meliboeus. Happy old man! So your land will still 46
be yours. And it's enough for you, even though the
bare rock and the marshland with its mud and reeds
encroach on all your pastures. Your pregnant ewes
will never be upset by unaccustomed fodder; no
harm will come to them through meeting other
people's flocks.

Happy old man! You will stay here, between the 51
rivers that you know so well, by springs that have
their Nymphs, and find some cool spot underneath
the trees. Time and again, as it has always done, the
hedge there, leading from your neighbour's land,
will have its willow-blossom rifled by Hyblaean bees
and coax you with a gentle humming through the
gates of sleep. On the other side, at the foot of the 56
high rock, you will have the vine-dresser singing to
the breezes; while all the time your dear full-
throated pigeons will be heard, and the turtle-dove
high in the elm will never bring her cooing to an end.

Tityrus. And so I say, stags must take wing and 59
feed in the upper air; the sea roll back and leave her
fishes high and dry; nations go wandering across
each other's lands, and Germans drink in exile from
the Tigris, or Parthians from the Saône – before the
memory of my patron's gracious look could vanish
from my heart.

Meliboeus. Yes, but meanwhile the rest of us are 64
off; some to foregather with the Africans and share
their thirst; others to Scythia, and out to where the
Oxus rolls the chalk along; others to join the
Britons, cut off as they are by the whole width of the
world. Ah, will the day come, after many years,
when I shall see a place that I can call my home, see

post aliquot, mea regna videns, mirabor aristas?
70 impius haec tam culta novalia miles habebit,
barbarus has segetes? en quo discordia cives
produxit miseros! his nos consevimus agros.
insere nunc, Meliboee, piros, pone ordine vites.
ite meae, quondam felix pecus, ite capellae.
75 non ego vos posthac viridi proiectus in antro
dumosa pendere procul de rupe videbo;
carmina nulla canam; non me pascente, capellae,
florentem cytisum et salices carpetis amaras.

TITYRUS

Hic tamen hanc mecum poteras requiescere noctem
80 fronde super viridi: sunt nobis mitia poma,
castaneae molles et pressi copia lactis;
et iam summa procul villarum culmina fumant
maioresque cadunt altis de montibus umbrae.

turf piled high on my poor cottage roof, and in due time survey with pride the modest crop that is my little realm?

Is some blaspheming soldier to own these acres I [70] have broken up and tilled so well – a foreigner, to reap these splendid fields of corn? Look at the misery to which we have sunk since Romans took to fighting one another. To think that *we* have sown, for men like that to reap! Yes, Meliboeus, now graft your pears; now plant a row of vines!

Forward, my goats; forward, the flock that used [74] to be my pride. Never again, stretched out in some green hollow, shall I spy you far away, dangling on the rocky hillside where the brambles grow. There will be no songs from me, my goats, and I shall lead you no more to crop the flowering clover and the bitter willow shoots.

Tityrus. Yet surely you could sleep here as my [79] guest for this one night, with green leaves for your bed? I have got ripe apples, and some mealy chestnuts and a good supply of cheese. See over there – the rooftops of the farms are already putting up their evening smoke and shadows of the mountain crests are falling farther out.

Tityrus — rustic, agricultural, satisfaction

Meliboeus — no farm, must fight for Rome + remain transient.

II

FORMOSUM pastor Corydon ardebat Alexim,
delicias domini, nec, quid speraret, habebat.
tantum inter densas, umbrosa cacumina, fagos
adsidue veniebat. ibi haec incondita solus
5 montibus et silvis studio iactabat inani.

'O crudelis, Alexi, nihil mea carmina curas?
nil nostri miserere? mori me denique coges.
nunc etiam pecudes umbras et frigora captant,
nunc virides etiam occultant spineta lacertos,
10 Thestylis et rapido fessis messoribus aestu
alia serpullumque herbas contundit olentes.
at mecum raucis, tua dum vestigia lustro,
sole sub ardenti resonant arbusta cicadis.
nonne fuit satius, tristes Amaryllidis iras
15 atque superba pati fastidia? nonne Menalcan,
quamvis ille niger, quamvis tu candidus esses?
o formose puer, nimium ne crede colori:
alba ligustra cadunt, vaccinia nigra leguntur.
despectus tibi sum nec, qui sim, quaeris, Alexi,
20 quam dives pecoris, nivei quam lactis abundans:
mille meae Siculis errant in montibus agnae;
lac mihi non aestate novum, non frigore defit.

THE PASSIONATE SHEPHERD
TO HIS LOVE

THE shepherd Corydon had lost his heart to the beautiful Alexis. But Alexis was his master's favourite. There was no hope for Corydon. His only comfort was to haunt the spots where the high beeches spread unbroken shade, and there, alone in idle ecstasies of love, he made the mountains and the woodlands listen to these disordered shreds of song: 6

'Cruel Alexis, do you care nothing for my songs? Have you no pity for me? You will end by driving me to death.

'This is the hour when even cattle seek the cool- 8 ness of the shade; when even the green lizard lies hidden in the thorny brake; when Thestylis brews a fragrant soup of pounded garlic and wild-thyme for the reapers wearied by the scorching heat. Yet I am wandering in the paths that you have trod, under the burning sun, while the orchards echo to the harsh cicadas' notes and mine.

'Would it not have been better to put up with the 14 sulky moods of Amaryllis and the airs she gives herself? Or with Menalcas, dark though he is – and you so fair?

'Beautiful boy, do not rely too much on lovely 17 colouring. The white flower of the privet falls: black bilberries are picked.

'Alexis, you despise me. You do not even ask 19 what sort of man I am, what flocks I may possess, how rich I am in snowy milk. Yet a thousand lambs of mine range the Sicilian hills; summer and winter I have fresh milk in plenty.

canto, quae solitus, si quando armenta vocabat,
Amphion Dircaeus in Actaeo Aracyntho.
25 nec sum adeo informis: nuper me in litore vidi,
cum placidum ventis staret mare; non ego Daphnim
iudice te metuam, si numquam fallit imago.
o tantum libeat mecum tibi sordida rura
atque humiles habitare casas et figere cervos
30 haedorumque gregem viridi compellere hibisco!
mecum una in silvis imitabere Pana canendo.
Pan primum calamos cera coniungere plures
instituit, Pan curat oves oviumque magistros.
nec te paeniteat calamo trivisse labellum:
35 haec eadem ut sciret, quid non faciebat Amyntas?
est mihi disparibus septem compacta cicutis
fistula, Damoetas dono mihi quam dedit olim
et dixit moriens "te nunc habet ista secundum".
dixit Damoetas, invidit stultus Amyntas.
40 praeterea duo, nec tuta mihi valle reperti,
capreoli, sparsis etiam nunc pellibus albo;
bina die siccant ovis ubera; quos tibi servo.
iam pridem a me illos abducere Thestylis orat;
et faciet, quoniam sordent tibi munera nostra.
45 huc ades, o formose puer: tibi lilia plenis

'And I can sing, as once upon a time Theban 23
Amphion used to sing when he was calling home
the cows on Attic Aracynthus.

'Nor am I as ill-favoured as all that. Down by the 25
sea the other day, I saw myself reflected when the
dying wind had left the water calm. You could compare me even with Daphnis, and I should have no
fears – if mirrors do not lie.

'If only you could bring yourself to live with me 28
under some humble roof in the homely countryside,
to shoot the stag, and drive a herd of goats with a
green marsh-mallow switch!

'With me beside you in the woods you will learn 31
to sing like Pan. Pan taught us how to join a set of
reeds with wax. Pan cares for sheep and for the
people who look after them.

'Nor let it vex you when you chafe your lip on a 34
reed. Amyntas shrank from nothing – he was so
keen to learn the secrets of the art.

'I have a pipe made of seven hemlock stalks of 36
graded length. Damoetas, long ago, as he lay dying,
made me a present of it. "You are its second slave,"
he said to me. That's what Damoetas said; and
Amyntas, like the fool he is, was jealous.

'Another thing – I found two little chamois in a 40
valley where a man might come to grief. They have
kept two white spots on their coats and twice a day
they suck the same ewe dry. I am saving them for
you, though Thestylis has long been pestering me
to let her have them.

'And so I shall, since you turn up your nose at all 44
my gifts.

'Ah, lovely youth, come here. Can you not see the 45

ecce ferunt Nymphae calathis, tibi candida Nais,
pallentes violas et summa papavera carpens,
narcissum et florem iungit bene olentis anethi;
tum casia atque aliis intexens suavibus herbis
50 mollia luteola pingit vaccinia caltha.
ipse ego cana legam tenera lanugine mala
castaneasque nuces, mea quas Amaryllis amabat;
addam cerea pruna: honos erit huic quoque pomo;
et vos, o lauri, carpam et te, proxima myrte,
55 sic positae quoniam suaves miscetis odores.
rusticus es, Corydon; nec munera curat Alexis,
nec, si muneribus certes, concedat Iollas.
heu heu, quid volui misero mihi? floribus Austrum
perditus et liquidis immisi fontibus apros.
60 quem fugis, ah, demens? habitarunt di quoque silvas
Dardaniusque Paris. Pallas, quas condidit arces,
ipsa colat: nobis placeant ante omnia silvae.
torva leaena lupum sequitur, lupus ipse capellam,
florentem cytisum sequitur lasciva capella,
65 te Corydon, o Alexi: trahit sua quemque voluptas.
aspice, aratra iugo referunt suspensa iuvenci,
et sol crescentes decedens duplicat umbras:

Nymphs, laden with baskets full of lilies – all for you? See the white Naiad, plucking, for you, pale irises and poppy-heads, binding narcissus to the fragrant anise-flower, with cassia and other scented herbs twined in, and flaming marigolds to make the modest blueberries look their best.

'Myself I'll pick you quinces with their white and 51 tender bloom, and the chestnuts Amaryllis loved when she was mine. And waxen plums. Yes; let the plum be honoured too.

'And I'll take toll of you as well, you laurels, and 54 your friends the myrtles. Set side by side you blend your perfumes very sweetly.

'Corydon, you're a clown. Alexis has no use for 56 gifts. And if you try to win him in that way Iollas will outbid you.

'Oh misery! What have I brought on my unhappy 58 self? My wits are gone: I have let the south wind dash my flowers, and had the wild-boars paddling in the clear water of my springs.

'Foolish Alexis, why should you run from a 60 countryman like me? There have been gods who made the woods their home. And so did Paris, Prince of Troy. Pallas can stay inside the citadels she builds for towns. I ask for nothing better in the whole world than the woods.

'The wild-eyed lioness pursues the wolf; the wolf 63 pursues the kid; the kid herself goes gambolling in search of flowering clover. And I chase you. Each is drawn on by what delights him most.

'I see the oxen pulling home the ploughs – their 66 yokes are set to lift the shares. And now the westering sun has doubled every shadow's length. But love still burns me up – and what can stop it?

'Corydon, Corydon, what is this madness that 69 has got you down? You have left your vines half-pruned and the elms they grow on thick with leaves. Rather than this, why not get busy on a useful piece of work and plait a basket with some osier-twigs or pliant reeds? If this Alexis treats you with contempt, you'll find another.'

Corydon's declaration of love for Alexis is linked to the rustic beauty and rustic optimism that Virgil symbolizes

III

ARE THESE MELIBOEUS' SHEEP?

Menalcas
Damoetas
Palaemon

III

Dic mihi, Damoeta, cuium pecus? an Meliboei?

Non, verum Aegonis; nuper mihi tradidit Aegon.

Infelix o semper, oves, pecus! ipse Neaeram
dum fovet ac, ne me sibi praeferat illa, veretur,
5 hic alienus oves custos bis mulget in hora,
et sucus pecori et lac subducitur agnis.

Parcius ista viris tamen obicienda memento.
novimus et qui te, transversa tuentibus hircis,
et quo (sed faciles Nymphae risere) sacello.

10 Tum, credo, cum me arbustum videre Miconis
atque mala vites incidere falce novellas.

Aut hic ad veteres fagos, cum Daphnidis arcum
fregisti et calamos: quae tu, perverse Menalca,
et cum vidisti puero donata, dolebas,
15 et si non aliqua nocuisses, mortuus esses.

Quid domini faciant, audent cum talia fures?
non ego te vidi Damonis, pessime, caprum
excipere insidiis, multum latrante Lycisca?
et cum clamarem 'quo nunc se proripit ille?
20 Tityre, coge pecus,' tu post carecta latebas.

An mihi cantando victus non redderet ille
quem mea carminibus meruisset fistula caprum?

Menalcas. Whose flock is that, Damoetas? Tell me, are these Meliboeus' sheep?

Damoetas. No; they are Aegon's. Aegon has just 2 left me in charge of them.

Menalcas. Poor sheep, unlucky all the time! Aegon 3 runs off to keep Neaera warm, fearing she may prefer me to himself, while here a hireling shepherd milks his ewes every half hour, till the whole flock is dry and the lambs are left without a drop.

Damoetas. Think twice before you bring that up 7 against a man. I know what *you* did, and the shrine you did it in. You made the very he-goats look askance. The Nymphs are tolerant: they only laughed.

Menalcas. Just as they did, of course, when they 10 saw me with a hook slashing at Micon's growing vines and vineyard trees!

Damoetas. Or here by the old beeches when you 12 smashed up Daphnis' bow and arrows, like the blackguard that you are. Why, you were in torment from the moment when you saw them given to the boy, and would have died if you hadn't managed to indulge your spite.

Menalcas. What can the farmers do, when thieves 16 become so bold? Did I not see you sneaking up to cut off one of Damon's goats? And when his mongrel barked and I called out, 'Tityrus, what is that villain after now? Better round up your flock!' there you were, skulking in the rushes.

Damoetas. Hadn't I beaten Damon in a match? 21 Hadn't my pipe and singing won me a goat from him? Why shouldn't he pay up? You may not know

si nescis, meus ille caper fuit; et mihi Damon
ipse fatebatur; sed reddere posse negabat.

MENALCAS

25 Cantando tu illum? aut umquam tibi fistula cera
iuncta fuit? non tu in triviis, indocte, solebas
stridenti miserum stipula disperdere carmen?

DAMOETAS

Vis ergo inter nos, quid possit uterque, vicissim
experiamur? ego hanc vitulam (ne forte recuses,
30 bis venit ad mulctram, binos alit ubere fetus)
depono: tu dic, mecum quo pignore certes.

MENALCAS

De grege non ausim quicquam deponere tecum:
est mihi namque domi pater, est iniusta noverca,
bisque die numerant ambo pecus, alter et haedos.
35 verum, id quod multo tute ipse fatebere maius,
(insanire libet quoniam tibi) pocula ponam
fagina, caelatum divini opus Alcimedontis;
lenta quibus torno facili superaddita vitis
diffusos hedera vestit pallente corymbos.
40 in medio duo signa, Conon et – quis fuit alter,
descripsit radio totum qui gentibus orbem,
tempora quae messor, quae curvus arator haberet?
necdum illis labra admovi, sed condita servo.

DAMOETAS

Et nobis idem Alcimedon duo pocula fecit,
45 et molli circum est ansas amplexus acantho,
Orpheaque in medio posuit silvasque sequentes;
necdum illis labra admovi, sed condita servo.

it, but that goat was mine. Damon himself admitted it to me, but said he could not pay.

Menalcas. You beat him in a match! I don't believe 25 you ever owned a set of reed-pipes joined with wax. All you were good for was to stand at the cross-roads and scrape a miserable tune out of one squeaking straw.

Damoetas. Right! Will you make a match of it and 28 see what each of us can do, singing in turn? I stake this heifer. Don't turn up your nose: she comes to the milk-pail twice a day and suckles a pair of calves as well. It's your turn now to name your stake.

Menalcas. I'm not like you: I dare not gamble on a 32 beast. I have a father and a spiteful step-mother at home. Twice every day both count the flock, and one of them counts the kids as well. No; since you are so set on this mad game, I name a stake which even you will grant is far more valuable – a pair of beechwood cups carved by the great Alcimedon himself. Embossed on each by his unerring knife there is a pliant vine, wreathing its scattered clusters with pale ivy. There are two figures in between: one 40 is of Conon, one of – who was the other sage who mapped the whole celestial sphere for mankind with his rod, and fixed the dates when we should reap or should bend our shoulders to the plough? I have not yet touched them with my lips: I keep them stowed away.

Damoetas. That same Alcimedon made a pair of 44 cups for me as well as you. He draped the handles with soft acanthus leaves, and in between put Orpheus and the trees coming after him. 'I have not yet touched them with my lips: I keep them stowed si ad vitulam spectas, nihil est quod pocula laudes.

MENALCAS

Numquam hodie effugies; veniam, quocumque vocaris.
50 audiat haec tantum – vel qui venit ecce Palaemon.
efficiam posthac ne quemquam voce lacessas.

DAMOETAS

Quin age, si quid habes; in me mora non erit ulla,
nec quemquam fugio: tantum, vicine Palaemon,
sensibus haec imis (res est non parva) reponas.

PALAEMON

55 Dicite, quandoquidem in molli consedimus herba.
et nunc omnis ager, nunc omnis parturit arbos,
nunc frondent silvae, nunc formosissimus annus.
incipe, Damoeta; tu deinde sequere, Menalca:
alternis dicetis; amant alterna Camenae.

DAMOETAS

60 Ab Iove principium, Musae: Iovis omnia plena;
ille colit terras, illi mea carmina curae.

MENALCAS

Et me Phoebus amat; Phoebo sua semper apud me
munera sunt, lauri et suave rubens hyacinthus.

DAMOETAS

Malo me Galatea petit, lasciva puella,
65 et fugit ad salices, et se cupit ante videri.

MENALCAS

At mihi sese offert ultro, meus ignis, Amyntas,
notior ut iam sit canibus non Delia nostris.

DAMOETAS

Parta meae Veneri sunt munera: namque notavi
ipse locum, aëriae quo congessere palumbes.

away!' One look at the heifer, and you'll say no more about the cups.

Menalcas. I swear that you shall not escape me 49 now. I am ready to meet you on whatever terms you choose. But we must have a judge ... Why, here's Palaemon. He will do. I am going to see that from today you never challenge anyone again.

Damoetas. All right, begin, if you have anything 52 to sing. I shall not keep you waiting. I am not going to run away from any judge. I only beg Palaemon, our good neighbour here, to listen to our songs with all his ears. This is a serious matter.

Palaemon. Sing on, then, since we are seated on 55 soft grass, and the year is at its loveliest, with growing crops in every field, fruit coming on every tree, and all the woods in leaf. Damoetas, you will lead off, and Menalcas follow, replying to you every time. Alternate song is what the Muses love.

Damoetas. Goddess of poetry, let us begin with 60 Jove. All the world is full of Jove. Earth owes its fruits to him. My songs are dear to Jove.

Menalcas. And I am dear to Phoebus. He loves the 62 laurel and the gently blushing hyacinth. I grow them always as a gift for him.

Damoetas. My Galatea is a saucy girl. She throws 64 an apple at me, then hides among the willows and hopes that I have seen her first.

Menalcas. Ah, but my sweet Amyntas comes to me 66 unasked. By now he is no more a stranger to my dogs than the Moon herself.

Damoetas. I have a present ready for my love. With 68 my own eyes I have marked the windy tree-top where the doves have built.

MENALCAS

70 Quod potui, puero silvestri ex arbore lecta
aurea mala decem misi: cras altera mittam.

DAMOETAS

O quotiens et quae nobis Galatea locuta est!
partem aliquam, venti, divum referatis ad auris.

MENALCAS

Quid prodest, quod me ipse animo non spernis, Amynta,
75 si, dum tu sectaris apros, ego retia servo?

DAMOETAS

Phyllida mitte mihi: meus est natalis, Iolla;
cum faciam vitula pro frugibus, ipse venito.

MENALCAS

Phyllida amo ante alias: nam me discedere flevit,
et longum 'formose, vale, vale,' inquit, 'Iolla'.

DAMOETAS

80 Triste lupus stabulis, maturis frugibus imbres,
arboribus venti, nobis Amaryllidis irae.

MENALCAS

Dulce satis umor, depulsis arbutus haedis,
lenta salix feto pecori, mihi solus Amyntas.

DAMOETAS

Pollio amat nostram, quamvis est rustica, Musam:
85 Pierides, vitulam lectori pascite vestro.

MENALCAS

Pollio et ipse facit nova carmina: pascite taurum,
iam cornu petat et pedibus qui spargat harenam.

DAMOETAS

Qui te, Pollio, amat, veniat quo te quoque gaudet;
mella fluant illi, ferat et rubus asper amomum.

Menalcas. I too have done my best. I have picked 70 ten golden apples from a tree in the woods and sent them to my dear. I'll send another ten tomorrow.

Damoetas. To think how often Galatea talks with 72 me! And ah, the things she says! Winds, carry some of them at least to the gods' ears.

Menalcas. I know, Amyntas, in your heart of 74 hearts you like me well. But how does that help me, if while you chase the boar I am left to mind the nets?

Damoetas. Let me have Phyllis with me for the 76 day, Iollas, since it is my birthday. When I am offering up a heifer for the crops, then come yourself.

Menalcas. Why, Phyllis is my dearest love! She 78 wept to see me go, and she lingered long on her 'Farewell, my beautiful Iollas!' and again 'Farewell.'

Damoetas. Wolves play the devil with the flocks; 80 rain with the ripened corn; gales with the trees; and Amaryllis's angry moods with me.

Menalcas. Showers are delicious to the springing 82 crops; arbutus to weaned kids; the bending willow to the mother goats. Only Amyntas pleases me.

Damoetas. Pollio loves my Muse, for all her 84 country ways. Pierian Maidens, make a heifer the reward for one who looks so kindly on your work.

Menalcas. Pollio does more: he is busy on new 86 poems of his own. Give him a bullock old enough to butt and kick the sand up with its heels.

Damoetas. May anyone who loves you, Pollio, 88 attain the heights that he is happy to have seen you reach. May honey flow for him, and prickly brambles yield Assyrian spice.

Menalcas. Mevius, I hope that anyone who can put 90 up with Bavius's verse may fall for yours. *And* let

MENALCAS

90 Qui Bavium non odit, amet tua carmina, Maevi,
atque idem iungat vulpes et mulgeat hircos.

DAMOETAS

Qui legitis flores et humi nascentia fraga,
frigidus, o pueri, fugite hinc, latet anguis in herba.

MENALCAS

Parcite, oves, nimium procedere: non bene ripae
95 creditur; ipse aries etiam nunc vellera siccat.

DAMOETAS

Tityre, pascentes a flumine reice capellas:
ipse, ubi tempus erit, omnes in fonte lavabo.

MENALCAS

Cogite oves, pueri: si lac praeceperit aestus,
ut nuper, frustra pressabimus ubera palmis.

DAMOETAS

100 Heu heu! quam pingui macer est mihi taurus in ervo!
idem amor exitium pecori pecorisque magistro.

MENALCAS

His certe neque amor causa est: vix ossibus haerent.
nescio quis teneros oculus mihi fascinat agnos.

DAMOETAS

Dic, quibus in terris (et eris mihi magnus Apollo)
105 tris pateat caeli spatium non amplius ulnas.

MENALCAS

Dic, quibus in terris inscripti nomina regum
nascantur flores, et Phyllida solus habeto.

PALAEMON

Non nostrum inter vos tantas componere lites:
et vitula tu dignus et hic – et quisquis amores
110 aut metuet dulcis aut experietur amaros.
claudite iam rivos, pueri: sat prata biberunt.

him harness foxes to the plough and milk he-goats!

Damoetas. You lads there, gathering flowers and 92
strawberries from their earthy beds, take to your
heels! There's a clammy snake lurking in the grass.

Menalcas. Sheep, do not venture out too far; it 94
isn't wise to trust this river-bank. Look at the ram
himself: his fleece is not yet dry.

Damoetas. Tityrus, head off your hungry goats 96
from the stream. When the time comes, I'll wash
them all myself at the spring.

Menalcas. Drive your flocks into the shade, lads. 98
If the sun gets at them and dries the milk, as it
did the other day, we shall be working at their
udders all for nothing.

Damoetas. It vexes me to see how lean my bull is, 100
there among the fattening vetch. Love is as fatal to
the herd as to the herdsman who looks after them.

Menalcas. My flock is suffering from something 102
even worse: they are all skin and bones. Some evil
eye must be bewitching these young lambs of mine.

Damoetas. Read me this riddle – and I shall take 104
you for Apollo's self. Where in the world is the sky
no more than three yards wide?

Menalcas. Answer me this – and Phyllis shall be 106
yours alone. Where in the world do flowers grow
with kings' names written on them?

Palaemon. It is beyond my powers to judge be- 108
tween you after such a duel. Both you, Damoetas,
and Menalcas here deserve to win a heifer. And so
do all who tremble at the approach of love's delight
or know its bitterness. Lads, drop the sluice-gates
now: the meadows have had enough to drink.

PP-4

> The bitterness of the dispute
> is absorbed under the common
> ground of mutual deserving,
> and both men are assuaged
> in their conviction by the beauty of nature.

IV

SICELIDES Musae, paulo maiora canamus.
non omnes arbusta iuvant humilesque myricae;
si canimus silvas, silvae sint consule dignae.
 Ultima Cumaei venit iam carminis aetas;
5 magnus ab integro saeclorum nascitur ordo.
iam redit Virgo, redeunt Saturnia regna;
iam nova progenies caelo demittitur alto.
tu modo nascenti puero, quo ferrea primum
desinet ac toto surget gens aurea mundo,
10 casta fave Lucina: tuus iam regnat Apollo.
teque adeo decus hoc aevi, te consule, inibit,
Pollio, et incipient magni procedere menses;
te duce, si qua manent sceleris vestigia nostri,
inrita perpetua solvent formidine terras.
15 ille deum vitam accipiet divisque videbit
permixtos heroas et ipse videbitur illis,
pacatumque reget patriis virtutibus orbem.
 At tibi prima, puer, nullo munuscula cultu
errantes hederas passim cum baccare tellus
20 mixtaque ridenti colocasia fundet acantho.
ipsae lacte domum referent distenta capellae

MUSES of Sicily, let us attempt a rather more exalted theme. Hedgerow and humble tamarisk do not appeal to all. If we must sing of woodlands, let them be such as may do a Consul honour.

We have reached the last era in Sibylline song. 4 Time has conceived and the great Sequence of the Ages starts afresh. Justice, the Virgin, comes back to dwell with us, and the rule of Saturn is restored. The Firstborn of the New Age is already on his way from high heaven down to earth.

With him, the Iron Race shall end and Golden 8 Man inherit all the world. Smile on the Baby's birth, immaculate Lucina; your own Apollo is enthroned at last.

And it is in your consulship, yours, Pollio, that 11 this glorious Age will dawn and the Procession of the great Months begin. Under your leadership all traces that remain of our iniquity will be effaced and, as they vanish, free the world from its long night of horror.

He will foregather with the gods; he will see the 15 great men of the past consorting with them, and be himself observed by these, guiding a world to which his father's virtues have brought peace.

Free-roaming ivy, foxgloves in every dell, and 18 smiling acanthus mingled with Egyptian lilies – these, little one, are the first modest gifts that earth, unprompted by the hoe, will lavish on you. The goats, unshepherded, will make for home with udders full of milk, and the ox will not be frightened

ubera, nec magnos metuent armenta leones;
ipsa tibi blandos fundent cunabula flores.
occidet et serpens, et fallax herba veneni
25 occidet; Assyrium volgo nascetur amomum.

At simul heroum laudes et facta parentis
iam legere et quae sit poteris cognoscere virtus,
molli paulatim flavescet campus arista,
incultisque rubens pendebit sentibus uva
30 et durae quercus sudabunt roscida mella.
pauca tamen suberunt priscae vestigia fraudis,
quae temptare Thetim ratibus, quae cingere muris
oppida, quae iubeant telluri infindere sulcos.
alter erit tum Tiphys, et altera quae vehat Argo
35 delectos heroas; erunt etiam altera bella
atque iterum ad Troiam magnus mittetur Achilles.

Hinc ubi iam firmata virum te fecerit aetas,
cedet et ipse mari vector, nec nautica pinus
mutabit merces; omnis feret omnia tellus.
40 non rastros patietur humus, non vinea falcem;
robustus quoque iam tauris iuga solvet arator;
nec varios discet mentiri lana colores,
ipse sed in pratis aries iam suave rubenti
murice, iam croceo mutabit vellera luto;
45 sponte sua sandyx pascentes vestiet agnos.

'Talia saecla' suis dixerunt 'currite' fusis

of the lion, for all his might. Your very cradle will adorn itself with blossoms to caress you. The snake will come to grief, and poison lurk no more in the weed. Perfumes of Assyria will breathe from every hedge.

Later, when you have learnt to read the praises of 26 the great and what your father achieved, and come to understand what manhood is, the waving corn will slowly flood the plains with gold, grapes hang in ruby clusters on the neglected thorn, and honey-dew exude from the hard trunk of the oak.

Even so, faint traces of our former wickedness 31 will linger on, to make us venture on the sea in ships, build walls around our cities, and plough the soil. With a new Tiphys at the helm, a second Argo will set out, manned by a picked heroic crew. Wars even will repeat themselves and the great Achilles be despatched to Troy once more.

Later again, when the strengthening years have 37 made a man of you, even the trader will forsake the sea, and pine-wood ships will cease to carry mer-chandise for barter, each land producing all it needs. No mattock will molest the soil, no pruning-knife the vine; and then at last the sturdy ploughman will free his oxen from the yoke. Wool will be taught no 42 more to cheat the eye with this tint or with that, but the ram himself in his own meadows will change the colour of his fleece, now to the soft glow of a purple dye, now to a saffron yellow. Lambs at their pastures will find themselves in scarlet coats.

The fates have spoken, in concord with the un- 46 alterable decree of destiny. 'Run, spindles,' they have said. 'This is the pattern of the age to come.'

concordes stabili fatorum numine Parcae.

    Adgredere o magnos (aderit iam tempus) honores,
cara deum suboles, magnum Iovis incrementum!
50 aspice convexo nutantem pondere mundum
terrasque tractusque maris caelumque profundum;
aspice venturo laetantur ut omnia saeclo!
o mihi tum longae maneat pars ultima vitae,
spiritus et, quantum sat erit tua dicere facta:
55 non me carminibus vincat nec Thracius Orpheus,
nec Linus, huic mater quamvis atque huic pater adsit,
Orphei Calliopea, Lino formosus Apollo.
Pan etiam, Arcadia mecum si iudice certet,
Pan etiam Arcadia dicat se iudice victum.
60 incipe, parve puer, risu cognoscere matrem:
matri longa decem tulerunt fastidia menses.
incipe, parve puer: qui non risere parenti,
nec deus hunc mensa, dea nec dignata cubili est.

Enter – for the hour is close at hand – on your [48] illustrious career, dear child of the gods, great increment of Jove. Look at the world, rocked by the weight of its overhanging dome; look at the lands, the far-flung seas and the unfathomable sky. See how the whole creation rejoices in the age that is to be!

Ah, if the last days of my life could only be prolonged, and breath enough remain, for me to chronicle your acts, then neither Thracian Orpheus nor [53] Linus could outsing me, not though the one had his mother and the other had his father at his side, Orpheus, his Calliope, and Linus, Apollo in all his beauty. If Pan himself, with Arcady for judge, were to contend with me, the great god Pan, with Arcady for judge, would own defeat.

Begin, then, little boy, to greet your mother with a smile: the ten long months have left her sick at [60] heart. Begin, little boy: no one who has not given his mother a smile has ever been thought worthy of his table by a god, or by a goddess of her bed.

Now! The Golden age in art returns, or so prophesy's Virgil.

V

MENALCAS

CUR non, Mopse, boni quoniam convenimus ambo,
tu calamos inflare levis, ego dicere versus,
hic corylis mixtas inter consedimus ulmos?

MOPSUS

Tu maior; tibi me est aequum parere, Menalca,
5 sive sub incertas Zephyris montantibus umbras,
sive antro potius succedimus. aspice, ut antrum
silvestris raris sparsit labrusca racemis.

MENALCAS

Montibus in nostris solus tibi certat Amyntas.

MOPSUS

Quid, si idem certet Phoebum superare canendo?

MENALCAS

10 Incipe, Mopse, prior, si quos aut Phyllidis ignes
aut Alconis habes laudes aut iurgia Codri.
incipe; pascentis servabit Tityrus haedos.

MOPSUS

Immo haec, in viridi nuper quae cortice fagi
carmina descripsi et modulans alterna notavi,
15 experiar: tu deinde iubeto certet Amyntas.

MENALCAS

Lenta salix quantum pallenti cedit olivae,
puniceis humilis quantum saliunca rosetis,
iudicio nostro tantum tibi cedit Amyntas.
sed tu desine plura, puer: successimus antro.

MOPSUS

20 'Exstinctum Nymphae crudeli funere Daphnim
flebant (vos coryli testes et flumina Nymphis),
cum complexa sui corpus miserabile nati

Menalcas. Mopsus, well met. We are experts, you and I – you with the light reed-pipe, and I at song. Why not sit down together here where the hazels mingle with the elms?

Mopsus. You are my senior. It is for me to follow 4 you, Menalcas, whether we go under the trees, where the fitful breezes make uneasy shade, or choose the shelter of the cave. Look at the mouth of it, half hidden by the scattered clusters of a woodland vine.

Menalcas. In all our hills, no one but Amyntas 8 claims to sing as well as you.

Mopsus. Maybe; but does he not claim also to out- 9 sing Apollo?

Menalcas. Lead off, Mopsus, with any song you 10 know. Let it be *Phyllis and her Loves*, or *In praise of Alcon*, or *Codrus Quarrelling*. Begin: our kids are feeding; Tityrus will keep his eye on them.

Mopsus. No; there's a song I wrote out the other 13 day on the green bark of a beech and set to music, marking the turns of voice and pipe. Let me try that one. Then you can tell Amyntas to compete!

Menalcas. If you ask me, Amyntas can stand up to 16 you no better than the bending willow to the olive in her tender green, or meek valerian to the crimson rose. But no more talk, my lad; we are here, inside the cave.

Mopsus. When Daphnis died – ah what a cruel 20 death! – the Nymphs lamented him. The very Nymphs (you hazels and you brooks will not deny it) wept as his mother threw her arms round the

atque deos atque astra vocat crudelia mater.
non ulli pastos illis egere diebus
25 frigida, Daphni, boves ad flumina; nulla neque amnem
libavit quadrupes nec graminis attigit herbam.
Daphni, tuum Poenos etiam ingemuisse leones
interitum montesque feri silvaeque loquuntur.
   Daphnis et Armenias curru subiungere tigres
30 instituit, Daphnis thiasos inducere Bacchi
et foliis lentas intexere mollibus hastas.
vitis ut arboribus decori est, ut vitibus uvae,
ut gregibus tauri, segetes ut pinguibus arvis,
tu decus omne tuis. postquam te Fata tulerunt,
35 ipsa Pales agros atque ipse reliquit Apollo.
grandia saepe quibus mandavimus hordea sulcis,
infelix lolium et steriles nascuntur avenae;
pro molli viola, pro purpureo narcisso
carduus et spinis surgit paliurus acutis.
40 spargite humum foliis, inducite fontibus umbras,
pastores (mandat fieri sibi talia Daphnis),
et tumulum facite et tumulo superaddite carmen:
"Daphnis ego in silvis, hinc usque ad sidera notus,
formosi pecoris custos, formosior ipse." '

MENALCAS
45 Tale tuum carmen nobis, divine poeta,
quale sopor fessis in gramine, quale per aestum

poor body of her son and taxed the gods and stars
with cruelty.

Nobody, Daphnis, drove the oxen from their 24
pastures to the cool stream in those sad days. Not
one beast drank a drop, or touched a blade of grass.

The very lions of Africa gave tongue – the moun- 27
tain jungle echoed their grief at Daphnis' death.

It was from Daphnis that we learnt to yoke Ar- 29
menian tigers to a car, and to lead the revellers in
the Bacchic dance, with vine-leaves dangling from
the supple rods we wave.

As the vine beautifies the elm, and grapes the 32
vine; as the bull ornaments the herd, and corn the
happy fields; so, Daphnis, you alone shed grace on
all about you.

When you were taken from us, Palēs herself with- 34
drew, and our own Apollo left the countryside. Too
often now, in furrows where we cast fat grains of
barley, the wretched darnel and the unprofitable
wild-oat spring up. Gone is the gentle violet, the gay
narcissus gone: thistles and prickly thorns rise up
instead.

Shepherds, strew leaves on the ground and screen 40
your springs from the sun – Daphnis demands these
rites. Build him a mound, and carve an epitaph on
top –

> *Countrymen, Daphnis is my name:*
> *The very stars have heard my fame.*
> *Here in the woods I lived and lie –*
> *My flock was lovely: lovelier I.*

Menalcas. My heaven-born poet! Your singing is 45
to me like sleeping on the grass when one is tired, or

dulcis aquae saliente sitim restinguere rivo.
nec calamis solum aequiperas, sed voce magistrum.
fortunate puer, tu nunc eris alter ab illo.
50 nos tamen haec quocumque modo tibi nostra vicissim
dicemus, Daphnimque tuum tollemus ad astra;
Daphnim ad astra feremus: amavit nos quoque Daphnis.

MOPSUS

An quicquam nobis tali sit munere maius?
et puer ipse fuit cantari dignus, et ista
55 iam pridem Stimichon laudavit carmina nobis.

MENALCAS

'Candidus insuetum miratur limen Olympi
sub pedibusque videt nubes et sidera Daphnis.
ergo alacris silvas et cetera rura voluptas
Panaque pastoresque tenet Dryadasque puellas.
60 nec lupus insidias pecori retia cervis
ulla dolum meditantur; amat bonus otia Daphnis.
ipsi laetitia voces ad sidera iactant
intonsi montes; ipsae iam carmina rupes,
ipsa sonant arbusta: "deus, deus ille, Menalca!"
65 sis bonus o felixque tuis! en quattuor aras:
ecce duas tibi, Daphni, duas altaria Phoebo.
pocula bina novo spumantia lacte quotannis
craterasque duo statuam tibi pinguis olivi,
et multo in primis hilarans convivia Baccho,
70 ante focum, si frigus erit, si messis, in umbra

slaking a noon-day thirst with a fresh draught from
a tumbling brook. Not only do you pipe, you sing,
as sweetly as your master did. Happy young poet!
His mantle falls on you.

Still, here's a song of my own I'll give you in 49
return, as best I may, raising your Daphnis to the
stars. Yes, I will set him there among the stars; for
Daphnis loved me too.

Mopsus. Could any kindness please me more? The 53
lad himself had earned a song; and Stimichon has
long been praising yours to me.

Menalcas. Clothed in new glory, Daphnis stands 56
at Heaven's Gate, where all is wonderful, watching
the clouds and stars below his feet.

It is for this that all things in the countryside, the 58
woods themselves, Pan and the shepherds, and the
Ladies of the Trees, are pierced with keen delight.

The wolves contrive no ambush for the flock; the 60
nets are innocent of guile towards the deer. Good
Daphnis stands for peace.

For very joy the shaggy mountains raise a clam- 62
our to the stars; the rocks burst into song, and the
plantations speak. 'He is a god' they say; 'Menalcas,
he is a god!'

Daphnis, be gracious to your friends and bring 65
them luck. See, there are four altars here. Two of
them shall be yours, two kept for sacrifices to
Apollo. Here, every year, I shall offer two cups
of fresh and foaming milk and two rich bowls of
olive-oil.

And best of all, we shall have merry-makings 69
where the wine will flow, in winter by the hearth, or
in the shade at harvest time. Our tankards shall be

vina novum fundam calathis Ariusia nectar.
cantabunt mihi Damoetas et Lyctius Aegon,
saltantes Satyros imitabitur Alphesiboeus.

    Haec tibi semper erunt, et cum sollemnia vota
75 reddemus Nymphis, et cum lustrabimus agros.
dum iuga montis aper, fluvios dum piscis amabit,
dumque thymo pascentur apes, dum rore cicadae,
semper honos nomenque tuum laudesque manebunt.
ut Baccho Cererique, tibi sic vota quotannis
80 agricolae facient; damnabis tu quoque votis.'

MOPSUS

Quae tibi, quae tali reddam pro carmine dona?
nam neque me tantum venientis sibilus Austri
nec percussa iuvant fluctu tam litora, nec quae
saxosas inter decurrunt flumina valles.

MENALCAS

85 Hac te nos fragili donabimus ante cicuta.
haec nos 'Formosum Corydon ardebat Alexim',
haec eadem docuit 'Cuium pecus? an Meliboei?'

MOPSUS

At tu sume pedum, quod, me cum saepe rogaret,
non tulit Antigenes (et erat tum dignus amari),
90 formosum paribus nodis atque aere, Menalca.

filled with the fresh nectar of the Chian grape. I will make Damoetas and Cretan Aegon sing. Alphesiboeus shall prance like any leaping Faun.

These rites are yours for ever, both when we pay 74 our duties to the Nymphs and when we bless the fields. So long as boars prefer the mountain-heights, and fish are true to water; so long as bees eat thyme and cicadas feed on dew – your name and dignities and praises shall survive.

Just as we do to Bacchus and Ceres, we country- 79 men will make you yearly vows. And you, like the other gods, will see that we fulfil them.

Mopsus. What can I do, what gift can I make you, 81 in return for such a song – sweeter, to my ear, than the music of the South Wind gathering way, or beaches beaten by the surf, or the streams that hurry down through rocky glens?

Menalcas. I will forestall you by giving you this 85 graceful reed – the very pipe to which I owe my *Passionate Shepherd and His Love*, the same that taught me *Are These Meliboeus' Sheep?*

Mopsus. And you must take his handsome shep- 88 herd's crook, with its even knots and studs of bronze. Many's the time Antigenes begged me for it. But though he was a lad in those days whom one well might love, he never got it. Menalcas, it is yours.

We praise Bacchus & Ceres
just as we do ~~B~~ Daphnies,
~~are~~ a terrific lyricist
that our Two characters admires

VI

Prima Syracosio dignata est ludere versu
nostra nec erubuit silvas habitare Thalia.
cum canerem reges et proelia, Cynthius aurem
vellit et admonuit: 'pastorem, Tityre, pingues
5 pascere oportet ovis, deductum dicere carmen.'
nunc ego (namque super tibi erunt, qui dicere laudes,
Vare, tuas cupiant et tristia condere bella)
agrestem tenui meditabor harundine Musam.
non iniussa cano. si quis tamen haec quoque, si quis
10 captus amore leget, te nostrae, Vare, myricae,
te nemus omne canet; nec Phoebo gratior ulla est,
quam sibi quae Vari praescripsit pagina nomen.
    Pergite, Pierides. Chromis et Mnasyllus in antro
Silenum pueri somno videre iacentem,
15 inflatum hesterno venas, ut semper, Iaccho;
serta procul, tantum capiti delapsa, iacebant
et gravis attrita pendebat cantharus ansa.
adgressi (nam saepe senex spe carminis ambo
luserat) iniciunt ipsis ex vincula sertis.
20 addit se sociam timidisque supervenit Aegle,
Aegle, Naiadum pulcherrima, iamque videnti
sanguineis frontem moris et tempora pingit.

THE SONG OF SILENUS

My earliest Muse, Thalia, saw fit to play with light Sicilian verse. She dwelt among the woods, and did not blush for that. Later, when kings and battles filled my thoughts, Apollo plucked my ear and gave me his advice. 'Tityrus,' he said, 'a shepherd ought to let his sheep grow fat, but court a slender Muse.'

Now, Varus, since bards enough will volunteer to 6 sing your praises and to compose the unhappy chronicles of war, I will take up my slender reed and practise the music of the countryside. I do not sing what I have not been bidden. Yet if these lines, such 9 as they are, should find a friend – should win one reader's heart – Varus, it will be you that all our tamarisks, every wood of ours, will celebrate. Indeed, no page could please Apollo more than one with *Varus* written at its head.

On, then, Pierian Maids!

Young Chromis and Mnasyllus came upon Silenus 13 lying asleep in a cave, and flushed, as usual, with yesterday's wine. The garlands had slipped off his head, but they lay there close beside it, and his heavy tankard hung by its handle from the fingers that had worn it thin. They closed with him (for the old man had often raised false hopes in both of them by promising to sing), and tied him up in the very garlands he had worn. Then, as they paused in alarm, 20 Aegle herself, the loveliest of the Naiads, came up to reinforce them and abet their deed, by staining the old man's brow and temples red with mulberry juice. He was awake by now, and smiling at their

ille dolum ridens 'quo vincula nectitis?' inquit.
'solvite me, pueri: satis est potuisse videri.
25 carmina quae voltis cognoscite; carmina vobis,
huic aliud mercedis erit.' simul incipit ipse.
tum vero in numerum Faunosque ferasque videres
ludere, tum rigidas motare cacumina quercus;
nec tantum Phoebo gaudet Parnasia rupes,
30 nec tantum Rhodope miratur et Ismarus Orphea.

Namque canebat, uti magnum per inane coacta
semina terrarumque animaeque marisque fuissent
et liquidi simul ignis; ut his exordia primis
omnia et ipse tener mundi concreverit orbis;
35 tum durare solum et discludere Nerea ponto
coeperit et rerum paulatim sumere formas;
iamque novum terrae stupeant lucescere solem,
altius atque cadant submotis nubibus imbres;
incipiant silvae cum primum surgere, cumque
40 rara per ignaros errent animalia montes.

Hinc lapides Pyrrhae iactos, Saturnia regna,
Caucasiasque refert volucres furtumque Promethei.
his adiungit, Hylan nautae quo fonte relictum
clamassent, ut litus 'Hyla, Hyla' omne sonaret.
45 et fortunatam, si numquam armenta fuissent,
Pasiphaën nivei solatur amore iuvenci.

ruse. 'Shackles!' he said. 'What for? Set me free, lads. You have proved that you could catch me: that is enough. Now you shall hear the songs you wish for. They are *your* reward. Aegle I will repay in other coin.' Then he began to sing, with no more said.

And now a miracle – you might have seen the 27 Fauns and the wild creatures dance lightly to the tune and stubborn oak-trees wave their heads. Rocky Parnassus is not so deeply moved by the music of Apollo; Ismarus and Rhodope have never known such ecstasy when Orpheus sang.

Creation was his theme – how elements of earth, 31 air, sea and liquid fire were massed together through the mighty void; how everything arose from these and the world itself, still soft, condensed into a globe. How next the land began to harden, to pen the Sea-god in his own domain, and slowly to assume the forms of things we know; how the first 37 glory of the new-born Sun struck the astonished Earth; how, when the clouds were raised and rain-showers had a longer fall, the woods began to grow, and one by one beasts made their devious way through wondering hills.

Then Pyrrha throwing stones behind her to make 41 men; the Reign of Saturn; and Prometheus tortured for his theft by eagles in the Caucasus. And Hylas – how the Argonauts had left the boy beside a spring, and shouted for him, till the long beach itself called 'Hylas', and again 'Hylas'.

So to Pasiphaë, a lady fortunate indeed if cattle 45 had never come into the world, but lost (the pity of it!) in her passion for a snow-white bull. Ill-starred

ah virgo infelix, quae te dementia cepit!
Proetides implerunt falsis mugitibus agros:
at non tam turpes pecudum tamen ulla secuta est
50 concubitus, quamvis collo timuisset aratrum
et saepe in levi quaesisset cornua fronte.
ah virgo infelix, tu nunc in montibus erras:
ille, latus niveum molli fultus hyacintho,
ilice sub nigra pallentes ruminat herbas,
55 aut aliquam in magno sequitur grege. 'claudite, Nymphae,
Dictaeae Nymphae, nemorum iam claudite saltus,
si qua forte ferant oculis sese obvia nostris
errabunda bovis vestigia; forsitan illum
aut herba captum viridi aut armenta secutum
60 perducant aliquae stabula ad Gortynia vaccae.'
    Tum canit Hesperidum miratam mala puellam;
tum Phaëthontiadas musco circumdat amarae
corticis atque solo proceras erigit alnos.
tum canit, errantem Permessi ad flumina Gallum
65 Aonas in montes ut duxerit una sororum,
utque viro Phoebi chorus adsurrexerit omnis;
ut Linus haec illi divino carmine pastor,
floribus atque apio crines ornatus amaro,
dixerit: 'hos tibi dant calamos, en accipe, Musae,
70 Ascraeo quos ante seni, quibus ille solebat

Pasiphaë, what madness seized you? Not one of Proetus' daughters, though they filled the fields with lowing like the cows they thought themselves, sank to such infamy and made a bull her mate. And yet they shrank, as cattle, from the yoke, and often felt for horns on their smooth brows. Ill-starred 52 Pasiphaë, roaming through the hills! Meanwhile your lover rests his snow-white flank on a soft bed of hyacinths, chewing the pale grass under a dark ilex-tree, or else pursues one of the many heifers of the herd. She calls to the spirits of the Cretan woods: 'Quick, Nymphs, and close the forest glades while 55 there is hope that I may light upon one imprint of that roving hoof. Maybe a bank of green grass took his fancy, or he may have kept up with the herd, and in the end be brought home by some heifers to the stalls at Gortyn.'

And then the maiden who coveted, too much, an 61 apple from the Gardens of the West; and the sisters of Phaethon, incased in moss and bitter bark, planted as alders, and made to shoot up from the ground.

Another scene – how Gallus wandering by the 64 waters of Permessus met a Muse, one of the Nine, who led him into the Aonian hills, where the whole choir of Phoebus rose as one in honour of the mortal man, and Linus, godlike singer of the countryside, whose head was garlanded with flowers and bitter parsley leaves, said to him: 'This reed- 69 pipe – take it from my hand – the Muses give to you; the very pipe they gave the Bard of Ascra long ago, which he played when he sang the stubborn ash-trees down the mountain-side. Sing to this pipe the

cantando rigidas deducere montibus ornos.
his tibi Grynei nemoris dicatur origo,
ne quis sit lucus, quo se plus iactet Apollo.'
    Quid loquar, aut Scyllam Nisi, quam fama secuta est
75 candida succinctam latrantibus inguina monstris
Dulichias vexasse rates et gurgite in alto
ah! timidos nautas canibus lacerasse marinis;
aut ut mutatos Terei narraverit artus,
quas illi Philomela dapes, quae dona pararit,
80 quo cursu deserta petiverit et quibus ante
infelix sua tecta super volitaverit alis?
    Omnia quae Phoebo quondam meditante beatus
audiit Eurotas iussitque ediscere laurus,
ille canit (pulsae referunt ad sidera valles),
85 cogere donec oves stabulis numerumque referre
iussit et invito processit Vesper Olympo.

tale of the Grynean Wood, till not a grove is left in which Apollo takes a greater pride.'

And must we follow him as he went on to sing of 74 Scylla, Nisus' child, whom story pictures as a lovely woman with a ring of howling monsters round her waist, harrying Odysseus' ships, and with her sea-dogs' fangs tearing the flesh (ah horror!) of his trembling men, down in the whirlpool's depths? Or as he sang of Tereus' altered shape, of the dish 78 that Philomela cooked for him, and the gift that followed it, of her swift flight into the wilderness, and of the unpractised wings on which the hapless Queen had hovered first above the roof-top that had once been hers?

Indeed, he gave them all the songs that once upon 82 a time Eurotas, happy river, heard from Phoebus' lips and bade his laurels get by heart. All these Silenus sang. The music struck the valleys and the valleys tossed it to the stars – till the lads were warned to drive home and to count their sheep, by Vesper, as he trod unwelcome into the listening sky.

Silenus knew Them all.

VII

THE SINGING-MATCH

Meliboeus
Corydon
Thyrsis

VII

FORTE sub arguta consederat ilice Daphnis,
compulerantque greges Corydon et Thyrsis in unum,
Thyrsis oves, Corydon distentas lacte capellas,
ambo florentes aetatibus, Arcades ambo,
5 et cantare pares et respondere parati.
huc mihi, dum teneras defendo a frigore myrtos,
vir gregis ipse caper deerraverat, atque ego Daphnim
aspicio. ille ubi me contra videt, 'ocius' inquit
'huc ades, o Meliboee: caper tibi salvus et haedi:
10 et si quid cessare potes, requiesce sub umbra.
huc ipsi potum venient per prata iuvenci,
hic virides tenera praetexit harundine ripas
Mincius, eque sacra resonant examina quercu.'
quid facerem? neque ego Alcippen nec Phyllida habebam,
15 depulsos a lacte domi quae clauderet agnos;
et certamen erat Corydon cum Thyrside magnum.
posthabui tamen illorum mea seria ludo.
alternis igitur contendere versibus ambo
coepere, alternos Musae meminisse volebant.
20 hos Corydon, illos referebat in ordine Thyrsis.

CORYDON

Nymphae, noster amor, Libethrides, aut mihi carmen
quale meo Codro concedite (proxima Phoebi

THE SINGING-MATCH

Meliboeus. As luck would have it, Daphnis had just sat down under a whispering ilex-tree, when Corydon and Thyrsis each drove up his flock to the same place, Thyrsis his sheep, and Corydon his she-goats with their udders full of milk – a pair of graceful lads, Arcadians both, and each as ready as the other to lead off with a song, or to give an apt response.

And now my own he-goat, the father of my flock, 7 who had slipped off as I was fencing young myrtles from the cold, went wandering up to them. Thus, I caught sight of Daphnis. He saw me too, and called across to me: 'Quick, Meliboeus, join us here. Your goat is safe; so are the kids. Rest in the shade, if you have time to spare. As for your bullocks, when they 11 want a drink, they will find their own way through the meadows to this very spot, where the Mincius embroiders his banks with a green fringe of bending rushes, and the sacred oak is loud with swarming bees.'

What ought I to have done? I had no Phyllis or 14 Alcippe to pen my new-weaned lambs at home. Yet Corydon and Thyrsis were bound to make a famous match of it. I put my business in the second place, and their amusements first.

So the pair set to, singing alternately against each 18 other. Their Muse insisted on this plan. Corydon sang his lines, and Thyrsis followed him in each case with an answering set.

Corydon. Nymphs of Libethrum, dearly loved by 21 me, either let me sing as you let Codrus sing, Codrus my friend, a poet second only to Apollo; or, if we

versibus ille facit); aut, si non possumus omnes,
hic arguta sacra pendebit fistula pinu.

THYRSIS

25 Pastores, hedera nascentem ornate poetam,
Arcades, invidia rumpantur ut ilia Codro;
aut, si ultra placitum laudarit, baccare frontem
cingite, ne vati noceat mala lingua futuro.

CORYDON

Saetosi caput hoc apri tibi, Delia, parvus
30 et ramosa Micon vivacis cornua cervi.
si proprium hoc fuerit, levi de marmore tota
puniceo stabis suras evincta coturno.

THYRSIS

Sinum lactis et haec te liba, Priape, quotannis
exspectare sat est: custos es pauperis horti.
35 nunc te marmoreum pro tempore fecimus; at tu,
si fetura gregem suppleverit, aureus esto.

CORYDON

Nerine Galatea, thymo mihi dulcior Hyblae,
candidior cycnis, hedera formosior alba,
cum primum pasti repetent praesepia tauri,
40 si qua tui Corydonis habet te cura, venito.

THYRSIS

Immo ego Sardoniis videar tibi amarior herbis,
horridior rusco, proiecta vilior alga,

cannot all attain such heights, I shall hang up my tuneful flute, here on this pine, and make the tree your own.

Thyrsis. Bring ivy-leaves to decorate your rising 25 poet, shepherds of Arcady, and so make Codrus burst his sides with envy. Or, if he tries to harm me with excessive praise, twine foxglove round my brows, to stop his evil tongue from hurting your predestined bard.

Corydon. Delian Maid, young Micon dedicates this 29 bristly boar's head and the branching antlers of a long-lived stag to you. And if this luck holds good, you shall stand here, carved in smooth marble, whole, with scarlet hunting-boots laced round your legs.

Thyrsis. This bowl of milk and these honey-cakes, 33 Priapus, are all you can hope for in the year, guarding a poor man's garden as you do. You are made of marble now – we can afford no more. But listen. If the flock multiplies at lambing-time, you shall be gold.

Corydon. My Galatea, Lady of the Sea, sweeter to 37 me than Hyblaean thyme, more lovely than pale ivy, brighter than any swan, come to me early, come when the bulls begin to leave their pastures for the byre, if your love, Corydon, is in your thoughts at all.

Thyrsis. Indeed now, you may think of me as 41 bitterer than Sardinian herbs, rougher than butcher's-broom, cheaper than sea-weed cast up on the beach, if this day has not been already longer than a year. Home with you, bullocks: you have had enough. Is there no shame in you? Home with you now!

si mihi non haec lux toto iam longior anno est.
ite domum pasti, si quis pudor, ite iuvenci.

CORYDON

45 Muscosi fontes et somno mollior herba,
et quae vos rara viridis tegit arbutus umbra,
solstitium pecori defendite: iam venit aestas
torrida, iam lento turgent in palmite gemmae.

THYRSIS

Hic focus et taedae pingues, hic plurimus ignis
50 semper et adsidua postes fuligine nigri:
hic tantum Boreae curamus frigora, quantum
aut numerum lupus aut torrentia flumina ripas.

CORYDON

Stant et iuniperi et castaneae hirsutae,
strata iacent passim sua quaeque sub arbore poma,
55 omnia nunc rident: at si formosus Alexis
montibus his abeat, videas et flumina sicca.

THYRSIS

Aret ager, vitio moriens sitit aëris herba,
Liber pampineas invidit collibus umbras:
Phyllidis adventu nostrae nemus omne virebit,
60 Iuppiter et laeto descendet plurimus imbri.

CORYDON

Populus Alcidae gratissima, vitis Iaccho,
formosae myrtus Veneri, sua laurea Phoebo:
Phyllis amat corylos: illas dum Phyllis amabit,
nec myrtus vincet corylos nec laurea Phoebi.

THYRSIS

65 Fraxinus in silvis pulcherrima, pinus in hortis,
populus in fluviis, abies in montibus altis:

Corydon. You mossy springs, and banks of grass 45 softer than sleep; you green arbutuses that cast the network of your shade across them; comfort our sheep under midsummer suns. The burning days are coming in and the buds already swelling on the tender shoots of the vine.

Thyrsis. Here is the hearth, logs rich in resin, a big 49 fire all the time, and doorposts blackened by the constant smoke. We care as little here about the North Wind and the cold as a wolf cares for numbers, or rivers for their banks in time of spate.

Corydon. Here prickly chestnuts stand, and junipers. 53 Everywhere the fruit lies strewn under its parent tree. The whole world smiles. But if the handsome Alexis were to leave our hills, you might see even the rivers running dry.

Thyrsis. The fields are parched, and the grass is 57 dying of thirst – it is this wicked weather! The Wine-god has begrudged the hillsides even the shadow that the vine-leaves gave. But when our Phyllis comes, the woods will all rejoice in green, and happy showers will fall in plenty from the sky.

Corydon. Hercules loves poplars best of all; 61 Bacchus prefers the vine; Venus, the Queen of Beauty, loves the myrtle best; and Apollo his own bays. Phyllis is fond of hazels. As long as Phyllis likes them best, neither the myrtle nor Apollo's bays shall take a higher place than hazels.

Thyrsis. The ash in forests is the loveliest tree; the 65 pine in gardens; the poplar by the river's bank; and the fir-tree on the mountain-heights. But if you, my handsome Lycidas, will spend more time with me,

saepius at si me, Lycida formose, revisas,
fraxinus in silvis cedat tibi, pinus in hortis.

MELIBOEUS

Haec memini, et victum frustra contendere Thyrsim.
70 ex illo Corydon Corydon est tempore nobis.

the ash in her own forest and the pine-tree in the garden must give place to you.

Meliboeus. So much I can recall. Thyrsis put up a 69 fight, but all in vain. He lost; and from that day it has been Corydon, Corydon every time with us.

Corydon won, but what a match.

VIII

Pastorum Musam Damonis et Alphesiboei,
immemor herbarum quos est mirata iuvenca
certantes, quorum stupefactae carmine lynces,
et mutata suos requierunt flumina cursus,
5 Damonis Musam dicemus et Alphesiboei.

Tu mihi, seu magni superas iam saxa Timavi,
sive oram Illyrici legis aequoris, – en erit umquam
ille dies, mihi cum liceat tua dicere facta?
en erit, ut liceat totum mihi ferre per orbem
[10 sola Sophocleo tua carmina digna coturno?
a te principium, tibi desinet. accipe iussis
carmina coepta tuis atque hanc sine tempora circum
inter victrices hederam tibi serpere laurus.

Frigida vix caelo noctis decesserat umbra,
15 cum ros in tenera pecori gratissimus herba,
incumbens tereti Damon sic coepit olivae.

DAMON

'Nascere, praeque diem veniens age, Lucifer, almum,
coniugis indigno Nysae deceptus amore
dum queror et divos, quamquam nil testibus illis
20 profeci, extrema moriens tamen adloquor hora.
incipe Maenalios mecum, mea tibia, versus.

DAMON AND ALPHESIBOEUS

DAMON and Alphesiboeus, singing in rivalry – let us record their pastoral melodies. A heifer heard their songs with such delight that she forgot to crop the grass; the very lynxes were bemused; and brooks, arrested, paused in their downward course. Damon and Alphesiboeus – let us commemorate the shepherds' Muse.

But where are you for whom I sing? Skirting, by 6 now, the mighty barrier of Timavus' rocks? Coasting the shores of the Illyrian Sea? . . . Ah, will the day ever come when I shall be allowed to chronicle your deeds? Will the day come when I can celebrate your tragedies, sole rivals of the Muse of Sophocles, through all the world? My first notes were inspired 11 by you: for you my last will sound. Accept this poem, begun at your command, and let its ivy twine with the victor's laurels round your brow.

It was the hour when the cold shade of Night has 14 scarcely faded from the sky, the time when dew on tender grass is most delicious to the sheep, that Damon chose to start his song, leaning against the smooth trunk of an olive-tree.

Damon. O Morning Star be born, and bring in 17 friendly day, while I, duped by my love for my unfaithful Nysa, make this lament and force the gods, though the vows they heard from us have brought me little good, to listen yet to the last utterance of one who will soon be dead.

Reed-pipe of Maenalus, support me in my song.

Maenalus argutumque nemus pinosque loquentes
semper habet, semper pastorum ille audit amores
Panaque, qui primus calamos non passus inertes.
25   incipe Maenalios mecum, mea tibia, versus.
Mopso Nysa datur: quid non speremus amantes?
iungentur iam grypes equis, aevoque sequenti
cum canibus timidi venient ad pocula dammae.
Mopse, novas incide faces: tibi ducitur uxor;
30 sparge, marite, nuces: tibi deserit Hesperus Oetam.
    incipe Maenalios mecum, mea tibia, versus.
o digno coniuncta viro, dum despicis omnes
dumque tibi est odio mea fistula, dumque capellae
hirsutumque supercilium promissaque barba,
35 nec curare deum credis mortalia quemquam.
    incipe Maenalios mecum, mea tibia, versus.
saepibus in nostris parvam te roscida mala
(dux ego vester eram) vidi cum matre legentem.
alter ab undecimo tum me iam acceperat annus,
40 iam fragiles poteram ab terra contingere ramos.
ut vidi, ut perii! ut me malus abstulit error!
    incipe Maenalios mecum, mea tibia, versus.
nunc scio quid sit Amor. duris in cotibus illum

On Maenalus the woods make music always and 22
the pine-trees speak. His hills for ever listen to the
loves of shepherd lads, and Pan himself, the first
that could not brook the silence of the reeds.

Reed-pipe of Maenalus, support me in my song.

So Nysa marries Mopsus! What may we lovers 26
not expect? Griffins will mate with mares, and, in
the years to be, the timid doe will come and drink
from the same basin as the hounds. Cut yourself
wedding-torches, Mopsus, for the bride is yours.
Fling nuts in the air, as bridegrooms do. It is for you
the Evening Star deserts his mountain bed.

Reed-pipe of Maenalus, support me in my song.

A worthy husband and a worthy bride! – Nysa, 32
who spurns the crowd; who loathes my flute, my
goats, my shaggy eyebrows and my straggling
beard; who thinks there are no gods to keep an eye
on what a woman does.

Reed-pipe of Maenalus, support me in my song.

You were a child, Nysa, when I saw you first – 37
you and your mother, gathering apples wet with
dew. It was in our garden, and I acted as your guide.
I was just tall enough to reach the laden branches
from the ground, though not yet twelve myself. At
the first look, I perished; at the first look, my soul
was lost to me.

Reed-pipe of Maenalus, support me in my song.

At last I know what Love is really like. That Boy 43
was never made of flesh and blood like us. His

aut Tmaros aut Rhodope aut extremi Garamantes
45 nec generis nostri puerum nec sanguinis edunt.
    incipe Maenalios mecum, mea tibia, versus.
saevus Amor docuit natorum sanguine matrem
commaculare manus: crudelis tu quoque, mater.
crudelis mater magis, an puer improbus ille?
50 improbus ille puer: crudelis tu quoque, mater.
    incipe Maenalios mecum, mea tibia, versus.
nunc et oves ultro fugiat lupus, aurea durae
mala ferant quercus, narcisso floreat alnus,
pinguia corticibus sudent electra myricae,
55 certent et cycnis ululae, sit Tityrus Orpheus,
Orpheus in silvis, inter delphinas Arion.
    incipe Maenalios mecum, mea tibia, versus
omnia vel medium fiat mare. vivite silvae;
praeceps aërii specula de montis in undas
60 deferar; extremum hoc munus morientis habeto.
    desine Maenalios, iam desine, tibia, versus.'
    Haec Damon: vos, quae responderit Alphesiboeus,
dicite, Pierides; non omnia possumus omnes.

ALPHESIBOEUS
'Effer aquam et molli cinge haec altaria vitta
65 verbenasque adole pingues et mascula tura,

cradle is the native rock, of Tmaros or of Rhodope, or the remote Saharan wilderness.

Reed-pipe of Maenalus, support me in my song.

Love has no pity in him. He taught a mother, 47 once, to stain her hands with her own children's blood. A cruel mother – yes; but was she worse than that remorseless Boy? A cruel heart indeed – but oh, the malice of the Boy!

Reed-pipe of Maenalus, support me in my song.

Now let the wolf, with none to drive him, fly in 52 panic from the lamb. Let the hard oak bring golden apples forth; narcissus bloom on alders; drops of rich amber sweat from tamarisk bark. Let the screech-owl outsing the swan; let Tityrus become an Orpheus, an Orpheus in the woods, or an Arion with the dolphins round him.

Reed-pipe of Maenalus, support me in my song.

No, let the deep sea overwhelm the world. Wood- 58 lands, good-bye to you; I will go up to the windy lookout on the mountain-top and plunge down headlong to the waves. Let Nysa take this last gift from a dying man.

Reed-pipe of Maenalus, be still: my song is done.

So Damon sang. What Alphesiboeus sang in 62 answer, it is for you to say, Pierian goddesses. We cannot all succeed in every task.

Alphesiboeus. Bring water out and wreathe this 64 altar with soft strands of wool. Burn rich vervain and manly frankincense, that I may see what sorcery

coniugis ut magicis sanos avertere sacris
experiar sensus; nihil hic nisi carmina desunt.

    ducite ab urbe domum, mea carmina, ducite Daphnim.
carmina vel caelo possunt deducere lunam,
70 carminibus Circe socios mutavit Ulixi,
frigidus in pratis cantando rumpiter anguis.

    ducite ab urbe domum, mea carmina, ducite Daphnim.
terna tibi haec primum triplici diversa colore
licia circumdo, terque haec altaria circum
75 effigiem duco; numero deus impare gaudet.

    ducite ab urbe domum, mea carmina, ducite Daphnim.
necte tribus nodis ternos, Amarylli, colores;
necte, Amarylli, modo et "Veneris" dic "vincula necto".

    ducite ab urbe domum, mea carmina, ducite Daphnim.
80 limus ut hic durescit et haec ut cera liquescit
uno eodemque igni, sic nostro Daphnis amore.
sparge molam et fragiles incende bitumine laurus.
Daphnis me malus urit, ego hanc in Daphnide laurum.

    ducite ab urbe domum, mea carmina, ducite Daphnim.

will do to stir that unimpassioned man of mine. Nothing is wanting here but magic spells.

> *Bring Daphnis from the town, my spells,*
> *bring Daphnis home.*

Spells can pull down the Moon herself from heaven. Circe with spells transformed Odysseus' men. Sing the right spell and you can blast the clammy snakes that live in the fields.

> *Bring Daphnis from the town, my spells,*
> *bring Dapnis home.*

I take three threads – three colours pick them out – and bind them round you first. Next, I walk round this altar with your effigy, three times. Odd numbers please the gods.

> *Bring Daphnis from the town, my spells,*
> *bring Daphnis home.*

Twine the three colours, Amaryllis, in three knots. Come, twine them, Amaryllis, and say: 'These are the chains of Venus that I twine.'

> *Bring Daphnis from the town, my spells,*
> *bring Daphnis home.*

This clay is hardened, and this wax is melted, by the selfsame fire. So may the fire of my love act on Daphnis. Scatter the salted grain and kindle crackling twigs of bay with pitch. The heartless Daphnis burns me up: I burn these bays to deal with *him*.

> *Bring Daphnis from the town, my spells,*
> *bring Daphnis home.*

85 talis amor Daphnim, qualis cum fessa iuvencum
   per nemora atque altos quaerendo bucula lucos
   propter aquae rivum viridi procumbit in ulva,
   perdita, nec serae meminit decedere nocti,
   talis amor teneat, nec sit mihi cura mederi.

90   ducite ab urbe domum, mea carmina, ducite Daphnim.
   has olim exuvias mihi perfidus ille reliquit,
   pignora cara sui: quae nunc ego limine in ipso,
   terra, tibi mando; debent haec pignora Daphnim.
      ducite ab urbe domum, mea carmina, ducite Daphnim.

95 has herbas atque haec Ponto mihi lecta venena
   ipse dedit Moeris (nascuntur plurima Ponto).
   his ego saepe lupum fieri et se condere silvis
   Moerim, saepe animas imis excire sepulchris
   atque satas alio vidi traducere messes.

100   ducite ab urbe domum, mea carmina, ducite Daphnim.
   fer cineres, Amarylli, foras rivoque fluenti
   transque caput iace, nec respexeris. his ego Daphnim
   adgrediar; mihi ille deos, nil carmina curat.
      ducite ab urbe domum, mea carmina, ducite Daphnim.

May Daphnis be possessed by such a yearning as a 85
heifer feels when, worn out by a long search for her
mate through copses and tall forest trees, she sinks
down on the green sedge by a running water, for-
lorn, forgetting even to go home as the dusk deepens
into night. May Daphnis know desire like that, and
I not care to cure it.

Bring Daphnis from the town, my spells,
bring Daphnis home.

Long since, the unfaithful wretch left in my hands 91
these things that he had worn, my sweet securities
for him. These pledges, Mother-Earth, I put into
your charge, here at my very gate. Daphnis is owing
to me on the strength of these.

Bring Daphnis from the town, my spells,
bring Daphnis home.

Moeris himself gave me these herbs and magic 95
simples gathered in the land of Pontus. They grow
in plenty there. Many's the time I have seen Moeris,
with their help, change into a wolf and vanish in the
woods. I have seen him call up ghosts from deep
down in the grave, and shift a standing crop from
one field to another.

Bring Daphnis from the town, my spells,
bring Daphnis home.

Up with the ashes, Amaryllis! Take them out, and 101
throw them over your shoulder into the running
water. But do not turn your head to look. It is
through them that I shall get at Daphnis – not that
he cares a jot about the gods or magic spells.

Bring Daphnis from the town, my spells,
bring Daphnis home.

Look, the whole altar is alight with flickering 105
flame! The ashes I was going to move have come to
life without my touching them. Ah, may this mean
good luck! Something will surely come of it. And
there is Hylax, barking at the gate. Can it be true?
Or is it nothing but a lover's fancy and an idle
dream?

Be still, my spells: he is coming from the town.
Be still now: he is here.

IX

LYCIDAS

Quo te, Moeri, pedes? an, quo via ducit, in urbem?

MOERIS

O Lycida, vivi pervenimus, advena nostri
(quod numquam veriti sumus) ut possessor agelli
diceret: 'haec mea sunt; veteres migrate coloni.'
5 nunc victi, tristes, quoniam Fors omnia versat,
hos illi (quod nec vertat bene) mittimus haedos.

LYCIDAS

Certe equidem audieram, qua se subducere colles
incipiunt mollique iugum demittere clivo,
usque ad aquam et veteres, iam fracta cacumina, fagos
10 omnia carminibus vestrum servasse Menalcan.

MOERIS

Audieras, et fama fuit; sed carmina tantum
nostra valent, Lycida, tela inter Martia, quantum
Chaonias dicunt aquila veniente columbas.
quod nisi me quacumque novas incidere lites
15 ante sinistra cava monuisset ab ilice cornix,
nec tuus hic Moeris, nec viveret ipse Menalcas.

LYCIDAS

Heu, cadit in quemquam tantum scelus? heu, tua nobis
paene simul tecum solacia rapta, Menalca!
quis caneret Nymphas? quis humum florentibus herbis
20 spargeret aut viridi fontes induceret umbra?
vel quae sublegi tacitus tibi carmina nuper,

THE ROAD TO TOWN

Lycidas. Moeris, where are you off to? This is the road to town. Is that where you are bound?

Moeris. Oh, Lycidas, a blow has fallen on us – one 2 we never even feared. That I should live to see a total stranger seize our farm and say, 'This is my property: be off!' – to us who have always worked the land! Now, we are a miserable, beaten crew; and, as would happen in this topsy-turvy world, it is for him that I'm taking in these kids – bad luck go with them!

Lycidas. But surely! I had heard that all the land 7 was saved, from where the hills fall back and leave a ridge to drop down with an easy slope, to the water and the old beeches with the battered tops – saved by your dear Menalcas and his poetry?

Moeris. No doubt you had. A rumour did go 11 round. But this poetry of ours, Lycidas, can do no more against a man in arms than the doves we have heard of at Dodona, when an eagle comes their way. In fact, if a timely raven on my left hand in the hollow ilex had not warned me at all costs to cut short this last dispute, neither your friend Moeris nor Menalcas himself would be alive today.

Lycidas. Could anyone conceive such wickedness? 17 To think, Menalcas, how near we came to losing you and, with you, all you did to cheer our lives! Who would have sung to us about the Nymphs? Who would have strewn wild flowers on the ground or given our springs green cover from the sun? Who else could have written the lines I overheard you sing the other day, quite unaware of me, as you

cum te ad delicias ferres, Amaryllida, nostras?
'Tityre, dum redeo (brevis est via) pasce capellas,
et potum pastas age, Tityre, et inter agendum
25 occursare capro (cornu ferit ille) caveto.'

MOERIS

Immo haec, quae Varo necdum perfecta canebat:
'Vare, tuum nomen, superet modo Mantua nobis,
Mantua vae miserae nimium vicina Cremonae,
cantantes sublime ferent ad sidera cycni.'

LYCIDAS

30 Sic tua Cyrneas fugiant examina taxos,
sic cytiso pastae distendant ubera vaccae:
incipe, si quid habes. et me fecere poetam
Pierides, sunt et mihi carmina, me quoque dicunt
vatem pastores; sed non ego credulus illis.
35 nam neque adhuc Vario videor nec dicere Cinna
digna, sed argutos inter strepere anser olores.

MOERIS

Id quidem ago et tacitus, Lycida, mecum ipse voluto,
si valeam meminisse; neque est ignobile carmen.
'huc ades, o Galatea; quis est nam ludus in undis?
40 hic ver purpureum, varios hic flumina circum
fundit humus flores, hic candida populus antro
imminet et lentae texunt umbracula vites:
huc ades; insani feriant sine litora fluctus.'

LYCIDAS

Quid, quae te pura solum sub nocte canentem
45 audieram? numeros memini, si verba tenerem.

were on your way to see our darling Amaryllis? –

Feed my goats, Tityrus, while I am gone – I shan't be 23 *long. And take them to the stream when they have fed. But watch the he-goat, Tityrus, as you go, and give him a wide berth. He is apt to butt.*

Moeris. Still better, though it isn't polished yet, 26 the poem to Varus that he was working on –

Varus, if only Mantua is spared to us – poor Mantua, 27 *too near for happiness to doomed Cremona – your name shall be extolled to heaven by our singing swans.*

Lycidas. Do lead off now, with anything of his 30 you know – and may your bees swarm on no Corsican yews; may your cows feed on clover till their udders cannot hold the milk. I too am a poet who has found some favour with the Muse. I too have written songs. I too have heard the shepherds call me bard. But I take it from them with a grain of salt: I have the feeling that I cannot yet compare with Varius or Cinna, but cackle like a goose among melodious swans.

Moeris. I am trying to please you, Lycidas. While 37 you were speaking, I have been cudgelling my brains in the attempt to recollect a song I knew – and not a bad one either –

Come here, my Galatea. What is there to amuse you in 39 *the sea? Spring, the gay spring, is here. Here by the stream all kinds of flowers are blooming on the turf. Here a bright poplar sways above my cave, and the dangling vines weave shadows on the ground. Come here, and let the wild waves hammer on the beach.*

Lycidas. What of the one I heard you sing to your- 44 self under a starry sky? I know the tune – if only I could recollect the words –

'Daphni, quid antiquos signorum suspicis ortus?
ecce Dionaei processit Caesaris astrum,
astrum, quo segetes gauderent frugibus et quo
duceret apricis in collibus uva colorem.
50 insere, Daphni, piros; carpent tua poma nepotes.'

MOERIS

Omnia fert aetas, animum quoque; saepe ego longos
cantando puerum memini me condere soles:
nunc oblita mihi tot carmina: vox quoque Moerim
iam fugit ipsa; lupi Moerim videre priores.
55 sed tamen ista satis referet tibi saepe Menalcas.

LYCIDAS

Causando nostros in logum ducis amores.
et nunc omne tibi stratum silet aequor, et omnes,
aspice, ventosi ceciderunt murmuris aurae.
hine adeo media est nobis via; namque sepulchrum
60 incipit apparere Bianoris: hic, ubi densas
agricolae stringunt frondes, hic, Moeri, canamus;
hic haedos depone, tamen veniemus in urbem.
aut si, nox pluviam ne colligat ante, veremur,
cantantes licet usque (minus via laedit) eamus.
65 cantantes ut eamus, ego hoc te fasce levabo.

MOERIS

Desine plura, puer, et quod nunc instat agamus.
carmina tum melius, cum venerit ipse, canemus.

Daphnis, why study the ascent of constellations that have 46
*had their day? See how Olympian Caesar's star has climbed
into the sky – the star to gladden all our corn with grain and,
paint the grapes with purple on the sun-bathed hills. Graft
your pears, Daphnis, now; your children's children will
enjoy the fruit.*

Moeris. Time carries everything away, even our 51
memory. How often as a boy I sang through the
long summer day and put the sun to bed! So many
songs forgotten! And now my very voice is failing
me. The wolves saw Moeris first. Well, never mind;
Menalcas will recite these poems to you to your
heart's content.

Lycidas. All this procrastination whets my appetite. 56
Now is the moment – look around! Through all its
length the lake lies calm and hushed for you; the
blustering wind has fallen: not a murmur left. Here
too we are just half-way: Bianor's tomb is coming
into sight. Here where the countrymen are thinning
out the leaves, here, Moeris, let us sing. Rest your 62
kids now, and we shall still reach town. Or, if it
looks as though the night might turn to rain before
we are in, why not go forward singing all the way?
It makes the going easier. I will relieve you of that
load; then we could walk and sing at the same time.

Moeris. No more, my lad. Let us stick to the 66
business in hand. As for Menalcas' songs, we shall
sing them all the better when he comes to us himself.

Torn from the land, it
is lovlier.

X

Extremum hunc, Arethusa, mihi concede laborem:
pauca meo Gallo, sed quae legat ipsa Lycoris,
carmina sunt dicenda: neget quis carmina Gallo?
sic tibi, cum fluctus subterlabere Sicanos,
5 Doris amara suam non intermisceat undam,
incipe; sollicitos Galli dicamus amores,
dum tenera attondent simae virgulta capellae.
non canimus surdis, respondent omnia silvae.

    Quae nemora aut qui vos saltus habuere, puellae
10 Naïdes, indigno cum Gallus amore peribat?
nam neque Parnasi vobis iuga, nam neque Pindi
ulla moram fecere, neque Aonie Aganippe.
illum etiam lauri, etiam flevere myricae,
pinifer illum etiam sola sub rupe iacentem
15 Maenalus, et gelidi fleverunt saxa Lycaei.
stant et oves circum. nostri nec paenitet illas,
nec te paeniteat pecoris, divine poeta:
et formosus oves ad flumina pavit Adonis.
venit et upilio, tardi venere subulci,
20 uvidus hiberna venit de glande Menalcas.
omnes 'unde amor iste' rogant 'tibi?' venit Apollo:
'Galle, quid insanis?' inquit. 'tua cura Lycoris
perque nives alium perque horrida castra secuta est.'

GALLUS

YET one more task, with your help, Arethusa, and I have done – a little poem to my beloved Gallus (who could refuse him that?), and for Lycōris too to read.

Begin, and may your stream slide under the 4 Sicilian waves unmingled with the harsh sea-brine. Begin, and let us tell the tale of Gallus' troubled love, while the snub-nosed she-goats crop the tender shoots. We are not singing to the deaf: the forest echoes every word.

Where were you, gentle Naiads, in what high 9 woods or in what glades, while Gallus lay dying of unrequited love? Nothing detained you on Parnassus; nothing on any ridge of Pindus; and nothing at Aonian Aganippe's spring. Yet even the laurels, even the tamarisks, wept for Gallus; for Gallus, lying by his lonely rock, even pine-clad Maenalus and the cold cliffs of Lycaeus wept.

The very sheep have gathered round. They think 16 no ill of us: think none of them, my heaven-born poet. Even the lovely Adonis grazed flocks along a stream.

The shepherd came; and the lumbering swine- 19 herds followed. Menalcas too, wet from gathering acorns in autumnal woods. All of them asked you: 'How did you come to lose your heart?'

Apollo came. 'Gallus,' he said, 'what madness is 21 this? Lycōris, your darling, has run off with another man, over the snows, to share the rigours of a soldier's life.'

venit et agresti capitis Silvanus honore,
25 florentes ferulas et grandia lilia quassans.
Pan deus Arcadiae venit, quem vidimus ipsi
sanguineis ebuli bacis minioque rubentem.
'ecquis erit modus?' inquit. 'Amor non talia curat:
nec lacrimis crudelis Amor nec gramina rivis
30 nec cytiso saturantur apes nec fronde capellae.'

Tristis at ille 'tamen cantabitis, Arcades' inquit,
'montibus haec vestris, soli cantare periti
Arcades. o mihi tum quam molliter ossa quiescant,
vestra meos olim si fistula dicat amores!
35 atque utinam ex vobis unus vestrique fuissem
aut custos gregis aut maturae vinitor uvae!
certe sive mihi Phyllis sive esset Amyntas
seu quicumque furor (quid tum, si fuscus Amyntas?
et nigrae violae sunt et vaccinia nigra),
40 mecum inter salices lenta sub vite iaceret;
serta mihi Phyllis legeret, cantaret Amyntas.
hic gelidi fontes, hic mollia prata, Lycori,
hic nemus; hic ipso tecum consumerer aevo.
nunc insanus amor duri me Martis in armis
45 tela inter media atque adversos detinet hostes:
tu procul a patria (nec sit mihi credere tantum)
Alpinas ah dura nives et frigora Rheni

Even Silvanus came, in all his woodland pride, 24
with flowering fennel and tall lilies nodding from
his head.

Pan came, the god of Arcady, as I myself have 26
seen him, stained with vermilion and with blood-
red elderberry juice. 'Enough, enough!' he cried.
'Love is not moved by such distress. You will no
more satisfy the cruel god with tears than goats with
leaves, or bees with clover, or the grass by water-
ing it.'

But Gallus, still disconsolate, said: 'Come what 31
may, you, my Arcadian friends, will sing of all this
to your hills – and what songs are there like the
songs of Arcady? How peacefully my bones would
lie, lulled by your reed-pipes making music of my
love! (unrequited).

'Indeed I wish I had been one of you, a shepherd 35
of your flocks, or a vineyard hand. Phyllis might then
have been my sweetheart, or Amyntas, or some
other love. And is Amyntas dark? Well, what of that?
Violets are dark, and so are blueberries. We should
have lain together, among the willows, under the
bending vines. Phyllis would have picked me garlands, and Amyntas sung for me.

'Here, my Lycōris, you would find cool springs, 42
soft meadows, woods. Here, with you by me, I
could endure the wastage of the years.

'But as it is, insensate loyalty to the stern god of 44
War keeps me in arms where weapons fly and the
enemy make their stand; while you (must I believe
such cruelty?) have left your country to set eyes,
alone, without me, on the Alpine snows and frozen

me sine sola vides. ah te ne frigora laedant!
ah tibi ne teneras glacies secet aspera plantas!
50   Ibo et Chalcidico quae sunt mihi condita versu
carmina pastoris Siculi modulabor avena.
certum est in silvis, inter spelaea ferarum
malle pati tenerisque meos incidere amores
arboribus: crescent illae, crescetis, amores.
55 interea mixtis lustrabo Maenala Nymphis,
aut acres venabor apros. non me ulla vetabunt
frigora Parthenios canibus circumdare saltus.
iam mihi per rupes videor lucosque sonantes
ire; libet Partho torquere Cydonia cornu
60 spicula. tamquam haec sit nostri medicina furoris,
aut deus ille malis hominum mitescere discat!
iam neque'Hamadryades rursus neque carmina nobis
ipsa placent; ipsae rursus concedite silvae.
non illum nostri possunt mutare labores,
65 nec si frigoribus mediis Hebrumque bibamus
Sithoniasque nives hiemis subeamus aquosae,
nec si, cum moriens alta liber aret in ulmo,
Aethiopum versemus oves sub sidere Cancri.
omnia vincit Amor: et nos cedamus Amori.'
70   Haec sat erit, divae, vestrum cecinisse poetam,
dum sedet et gracili fiscellam texit hibisco,
Pierides; vos haec facietis maxima Gallo,

Rhine. Ah, may the frost not hurt you; may the sharp ice not cut your dainty feet!

'I will go now and tune to the Sicilian shepherd's 50 pipe the poems I once wrote in Chalcidic verse. I am resolved: I choose the hard life in the forest, where the wild beasts have their caves. I'll carve my love on sapling trees: as the trees grow, so will my love. 55 And I meanwhile will wander with the Nymphs on Maenalus, or hunt the savage boar. No frost shall hinder me from drawing coverts on Parthenius with my hounds. I see myself already, climbing the crags; I hear the echoes as I thread the woods; a Cretan arrow flies from my Parthian bow – and I am happy.

'As though such things could be a cure for my 60 disease! As though the god of Love could soften to the sufferings of men! No; all is over. Tree-nymphs and poetry itself have ceased to please. Even you have failed, woodlands; away with you! Nothing I might endure could change a god like 64 him – not if I were to face the sleet and snow of Macedonian skies and drink from the Hebrus in midwinter weather; not if I chose, when the dry bark hangs dying on the elms, to shepherd Ethiopian sheep under the tropic sun. Love carries all before him: I too must yield to Love.'

Pierian goddesses, let these lines suffice for your 70 poet to have sung, as he sat and wove a basket with slim marsh-mallow twigs. I count on you to make the most of them to Gallus – Gallus, my love for whom grows as much hour by hour as the green alder shoots up when the spring is young.

Now let us go. The shade is bad for singers. This 75

Gallo, cuius amor tantum mihi crescit in horas,
quantum vere novo viridis se subicit alnus.
75 surgamus: solet esse gravis cantantibus umbra,
iuniperi gravis umbra, nocent et frugibus umbrae.
ite domum saturae, venit Hesperus, ite capellae.

is a juniper: its shade is bad. Even crops suffer in the shade.

Home with you, goats: you have had your fill. 77
Hesper is coming: home with you, goats.

ESSAYS ON THE ECLOGUES

*

GLOSSARY

I

THE DISPOSSESSED

'I sang of you, Tityrus, under the awning of a spreading beech.'   *Georgics*, IV, 566.

IN the first words of the First Eclogue, Virgil sounds the keynote of the whole work. With Tityrus practising woodland melodies on his pipe, he invites us into the Arcady that he has seen. But a conflicting note follows fast on the first theme. With 'Exile for me, Tityrus', we are once more in touch with the world of fact – a world less real than the other, if reality can be held to admit of degrees, yet persistently intrusive none the less. The conflict between these two themes makes a beautiful poem of what might only have been a pretty one.

It means also that to appreciate the poem we should know something of its setting and understand the circumstances in which Meliboeus has just been ousted from his farm, while the more fortunate Tityrus is left in possession of his meagre holding by the authorities in Rome. Nor have the critics ever stopped asking whether Virgil imagined this little drama in a spirit of altruistic sympathy with the Italian countryman's passionate attachment to the soil, or whether he wishes us to understand that he is recording experiences of his own. In other words, is Virgil either 'Tityrus' or 'Meliboeus' in this Eclogue, and 'Menalcas' in the Ninth, or is he no more than the creator of all three characters?

The evictions were real enough. They occurred all too frequently during the period of civil war that followed the assassination of Julius Caesar in 44 B.C. Virgil's native province in Northern Italy suffered heavily at the hands of the Commissioners appointed by Octavian (the future Emperor Augustus) to find lands for the settlement of his discharged veterans; and the territories of Cremona, with some of the farmlands of its neighbour Mantua, were seized for this purpose after his victory over Brutus and Cassius at Philippi in 42 B.C.

But that, I think, is all we need to know of contemporary events in order to enjoy the poem, and all that Virgil himself intended us to bear in mind when reading it. I do not believe that he wished us to take either Tityrus or Meliboeus for himself. He is their creator. If he is either, he is both of them – Tityrus singing for ever under the spreading beech and Meliboeus never ceasing to lament for his once prosperous flock.

Yet, since most of the scholars have not been content to leave it at that, we should perhaps examine a little more closely the personal and historical problems which a different reading of the Eclogue raises, admitting that we should be glad to glean from it any facts of Virgil's external life that can be legitimately inferred.

First then, is there anything to prove that Virgil or his family did lose their Mantuan farm in the course of these high-handed proceedings? The only contemporary evidence outside the *Eclogues* is a little poem[1] by the youthful Virgil himself, clearly written at a distance from home (possibly at Naples) and

1. *Villula quae Sironis eras*, etc. I should add that it is by no means universally accepted as genuine.

suggesting that some calamity was threatening his father in their home province. We have to wait a long time before this very meagre clue is supplemented. The later evidence is gleaned from a life of Virgil compiled by Probus, possibly in Nero's reign; an epigram by Martial, who wrote under Domitian; another *Life*, known as that of Donatus, which probably originated with Suetonius in the time of Hadrian; and finally from the much later commentators known as Donatus and Servius. Probus tells one story, Martial another, and Suetonius combines and confuses the two. The later biographers, who drew on Suetonius, only add further complexity and uncertainty to the tale – not unnaturally, since, in my opinion, they and their predecessors all went for their details to the poems themselves, and these, however closely questioned, give us anything but a straightforward and unified account. We shall never know the facts. And even if we did know that the farm was seized, we might still be wrong in thinking that Virgil, in this Eclogue and the Ninth, is recording his own experiences, rather than giving an impersonal but sympathetic picture of the husbandmen's difficulties in troubled times.

However, the tale, for what it is worth, runs roughly as follows. Virgil is Tityrus in the First Eclogue and Menalcas in the Ninth. After an unsuccessful petition presented to the authorities in poetical form, he is deprived of his ancestral lands by one or other of three Commissioners, Pollio, Varus, and Gallus; travels to Rome in search of restitution; and obtains it from Octavian, who causes one of the three to rescind the eviction order made

by his colleague or predecessor. Further, on returning north to resume possession, he is attacked by the
new occupant (a centurion named Arrius in some
accounts), and saves his life only by plunging into
the River Mincius and swimming to the farther
bank.[1]

As I have already suggested, this circumstantial
though varied account can, if one is in the right
mood for the task, be built up readily from the
poems themselves, even to the last picturesque
detail, which is founded on the incident in the Third
Eclogue where the ram gets a wetting in the stream.
But I must warn the reader that if he takes this
allegorical view of the *Eclogues*, he will not have an
easy case to handle. Indeed it is beset with assump-
tions and difficulties.

For instance, it is only guesswork to identify with
Mantua the market town that the shepherds refer to
as their own. They do not name it. It is also an
assumption, though perhaps a more likely one, that
the 'god' who gives Tityrus his blessing in Rome is
to be taken for Octavian. Then there is the question
of Virgil's pseudonyms. On a special occasion, in
the Sixth Eclogue, he does for once call himself
Tityrus; so there is some reason for thinking that
the young poet may be the greybeard Tityrus in the
First. But, if so, he saves his farm; whereas, if we
allow him by some caprice to have become Menalcas
in the Ninth, the farm is lost. So why not make him
Meliboeus here? If we do that, we shall at any rate
have lost his farm for him, as we set out to do. And
three different disguises in a single book are scarcely

1. See also p. 134.

worse than two. The alternative is to suppose that in the course of a few pages he congratulates himself on the restitution of his farm and condoles with himself on its loss – which would at least be odd, though perhaps not impossible.

But real absurdity is achieved when the critics, forgetting that the allegory is an assumption of their own, round on the innocent Virgil for describing *himself* as going to Rome in two inconsistent capacities, as a land-owner, to recover his farm, and as a serf, to purchase his freedom.

My net feeling is that Virgil is not reporting his own or his father's misfortunes. He is certainly referring to contemporary events, and he may be transmuting his experience of life, as poets will; for even the most imaginative writer must at some point make his contacts with external reality. But further than this, I for one, feel that we must not go.

After digressing on these problems at perhaps too great a length, I will add nothing to what I have already said about the beauty of this moving poem, lest I explain it all away. I will even leave the reader to discover Tennyson's indebtedness to Virgil by himself. But a word on the topography of the *Eclogues* will not come amiss at this point.

Their scenery was for a long time held to be composite. Here, for instance, the beech trees, the mountains and the high rocks suggest the Sicilian landscape, while on the other hand the marshy surroundings of the little farm are more typical of the valley of the River Po in Northern Italy. But R. S. Conway made out a strong case for the poet's accuracy in his Harvard Lecture, *Where Was Virgil's*

Farm? and convinced some scholars that he is faithfully describing the country round his own birthplace, in a village near the foothills of the Alps and at a greater distance from the low-lying town of Mantua than had hitherto been supposed. On the other hand, Tenney Frank, in his *Vergil: A Biography*, maintains that the poet wrote at Naples and that the scenery of his pastoral poems is for the most part Neapolitan. The latest contribution to the problem comes from H. J. Rose, who, in his recent book, *The Eclogues of Vergil*, suggests that the poet is in the main relying on memories of summer holidays spent with the shepherds in their *highland* pastures in the lower Alps. This, in my opinion, comes nearer to the truth. Virgil, as poets often do, wrote from his memory and his imagination. His scenes have a natural consistency, but he is no more to be cross-examined on topographical details than is Housman in his *Shropshire Lad*.

Whatever they may make of these divergent views of the scenery of the *Eclogues*, British readers will be amused to see their own country referred to in terms that they themselves might use of Tierra del Fuego. When Virgil wrote, Britain had not yet been brought within the confines of the Roman Empire. Julius Caesar had made a landing there in 55 B.C., and a reconnaissance in force in 54, but on each occasion our forefathers had acquitted themselves against him with their usual obstinacy; and it was not till much later, under the Emperor Claudius, that the island, or rather its southern part, was overrun and occupied by the Roman legions.

II

THE PASSIONATE SHEPHERD
TO HIS LOVE

In the Second Eclogue, Virgil has set himself the difficult task of creating a unified poem out of what he himself describes as 'shreds of song'. And these must be 'disordered' – or he departs from his own programme. The skill by which each disjointed utterance is made to lead into the next, each intervening thought is left unspoken yet revealed, so that the completed chain emerges as an integral whole, is consummate.

The Eclogue is exceptional too in another respect. Elsewhere for the most part, when the sun begins to overpower us, we are led under the shadow of the leafy trees or into the still cooler recesses of a mossy cavern. But here, with Corydon in his lovelorn rambles, we are exposed to the blistering heat of the summer sun, while the high, insistent, drumming of the cicada dins our ears.

But most of the critics, at any rate up to the end of the 19th century, seem not so much concerned with Virgil's poetical achievement as with the ethical questions raised by his choice of a subject. Servius, writing long before our own Shakespeare addressed sonnets to a youth, and imbued with the idea that a poet is generally to be identified with one of the characters whose feelings he describes, makes no bones of the matter at all. According to him, Corydon is Virgil; and Virgil loved a youth called

Alexander (disguised here as Alexis), whom his friend Pollio gave him at a dinner-party after Virgil had complimented him on the lad's good looks. Servius has the grace to add that there was nothing reprehensible about this affection.

Conington, in commenting on this Eclogue in connexion with Servius's gossip, makes a remark which I quote as typical of Victorian criticism at its most pompous and obtuse. 'We should be glad,' he says, 'to believe it to be purely imaginary, though even then it is sufficiently degrading to Virgil.'[1] On the other hand, Sellar, in his book on the poet, will have none of this nonsense. He appeals on behalf of Virgil's morals to the unanimous opinion of his friends and to the impression of integrity and purity which his work makes on our minds. Wordsworth's appreciation too is reassuring.[2] And so is Macaulay's. The latter not only preferred the *Eclogues* to the *Georgics* and the *Aeneid*, but of the Eclogues he liked the Tenth and Second best. We can surely accept without qualms what Lord Macaulay blessed, and leave Virgil's reputation in these able hands.

However, it will not be out of place to add a word or two here on what the Greeks and Romans have to say about the passion of love. To them, if we may take their more thoughtful writers as representing the best public opinion, love was a divine pheno-

---

1. John Conington, *The Works of Virgil*, Vol. 1 (1858).

2. W. Y. Sellar (*Virgil*, p. 172) quotes from S. Coleridge's *Memoirs*, Vol. 11, p. 411 as follows: 'I am much pleased to see (writes S. Coleridge), how highly Mr Wordsworth speaks of Virgil's style, and of his Bucolics, which I have ever thought most graceful and tender. They are quite another thing from Theocritus however they may be based on Theocritus.'

menon, whatever form it took, an ecstasy to be studied dispassionately, though not without awe, as the visitation of a powerful influence external to man. They expressed this feeling by making the goddess Aphrodite and her son Eros (the Roman Venus and her son Cupid) responsible between them for all that happens in the poor lover's heart. Homer, in Book XXIII of the *Odyssey*, causes Penelope, the constant queen, to excuse or at least condone the infidelity of the notorious Helen by attributing her infatuation to the temptation of the goddess. Sophocles's most memorable epithet of Eros is 'unconquerable in battle'. Virgil himself, when dealing, in the Sixth Eclogue, with a far more abnormal attachment than that of Corydon, the legendary Pasiphaë's passion for a bull, hastens to commiserate the ill-starred lady before he contrasts her infamy with the integrity of Proetus' daughters. And again, in the Eighth, we hear how Cupid 'taught' Medea, still in love with the faithless Jason, to murder the children she had borne him; and Virgil leaves us in doubt which of the two, Medea or the god, he thinks is most to blame.

But no Greek or Roman writer presents the whole picture so clearly as does Plato in his *Symposium*. Here love is studied in its upward progress from the lowest to the highest threshold, and looking through the philosopher's eyes we learn to appreciate the Greek idea that in all love, however mundane, provided it be absolute and self-obliterating, there lurks a divine spark which shows its kinship with the consuming fire that is the love of God.

III

ARE THESE MELIBOEUS' SHEEP?

'Alternate song delights the Muse.'
Eclogue III, 59

SERVIUS, though he seems not to rank the rather acrimonious Third Eclogue as high as some of the others, is yet careful to point out that variety is the essence of pastoral poetry and that Virgil was justified in enriching his collection by adding to it this picture of his shepherd songsters in less genial mood. I think we may be even more grateful to Virgil than Servius suggests. The whole poem goes with a swing. Not only is the preliminary backchat of the shepherds both fast and entertaining but when they at last settle down to their duel, we enjoy a delightful combat of wits, with a subtlety and speed of thrust and parry that challenge the closest attention. Moreover, in this and the Seventh Eclogues, we feel that Virgil comes nearer than in any other part of his book to the type of extemporary contest with which we can suppose the real shepherds of the ancient world to have amused themselves during the long days they spent among Arcadian or Sicilian hills.

In such contests, for which the technical term is amoebaean, one of the singers leads off with a short song of a few lines on a theme of his own choice, and is immediately followed by his rival with an utterance of equal length on the same or a contrasted theme, designed to cap, refute, or in some way improve upon the lines it answers. The first singer then proceeds either to open another aspect of the theme, or to broach a new topic, which his opponent must deal with as before. One would have thought that the challenger would be handicapped by being allotted the second place, which must surely have taxed the invention and wit of the contestants far more than the first. But this was not so. Here, for instance, Damoetas, the challenger, though he offers to waive his right to the first place, is ordered by the umpire to begin.

Amoebaean singing must indeed have been a difficult and a fascinating art. Today it is still true that 'alternate song delights the Muse': we have it yet in several forms. But alternate *improvization* is another matter, and I know of no school of modern singers or crooners whose efforts in that direction I am anxious to hear. On the other hand I am told by members of our forces who have been in Cyprus that the art is still practised and held in high esteem in that island.

The little songs themselves were of course for the most part dramatic in form. I mean that the singer, like any modern entertainer, sang, as often as not, in an assumed rôle, as when Menalcas answers Damoetas's request to Iollas for the loan of Phyllis with an indignant reply in the name of Iollas himself. The settings too are imaginary. Damoetas's sudden discovery of a snake in the grass is *not* a signal for his audience to disperse.

Unfortunately, these facts, so obvious that I hesitated to mention them, have afforded encourage-

ment once more to the commentators who find
hidden meanings in all these poems of Virgil. For
instance, Servius, not content to let Menalcas recall
an occasion when the ram of his flock has ventured
too near the river-bank and fallen in, tells us that the
shepherd is speaking for Virgil and referring to the
alleged fact that the poet escaped from the centurion
who had seized his farm only by plunging into the
River Mincius. At the same time it must be said on
Servius's behalf that he can administer a neat rebuke
when he detects his own foible in others. To those
who would have us read into Menalcas's gift of ten
apples to his love Virgil's dedication of his ten
Eclogues to Augustus, he tartly replies: 'A super-
fluous suggestion. Why drag in allegory here?' And
he scores too when he points out how Palaemon
stems the flow of song from the two lads by the
timely 'allegory' of his concluding words.

However there certainly are some places in the
poem where we must allow that Virgil has caused
his shepherds to express his own opinions; for
instance where he compliments his friend and patron
Pollio as a critic and a poet; and where he rounds on
Mevius and Bavius, two contemporary writers of
whom we know little more than that they had
ventured to disparage his work.

Finally, there are the two riddles with which the
contest comes to an end. Here, at the risk of dis-
appointing crossword addicts, I am going to fall
back on the naive comment that Servius makes
(after cataloguing a number of peculiarly unsatis-
factory answers). 'It must,' he says, 'be admitted
that, like most others, these enigmas do not lend

themselves to any obvious solution.' He also tells us that Virgil was reported to have said, with reference to the first of them, that he had 'set a trap for the scholars'. If that is so, I hope to be excused if I give it a wide berth.

IV

THE GOLDEN AGE RETURNS

'What could I not have made of you, if I had found
you still alive?'
*Words put into the mouth of St Paul, standing before
Virgil's tomb at Naples, by an unknown Christian poet.*

No short poem in any language has been so much
discussed as the Fourth Eclogue. In a brief essay
one can do little more than suggest the fascination
and the complexity of the controversies it has
aroused.

Our best approach to them will be to review, in a
simplified form, the three main interpretations that
can be put upon the poem – the lyrical, the political,
and the Messianic.

I

First, then, it is not impossible to accept the
Eclogue simply as a lyrical utterance, a poet's
expression of delight at the prospect of returning
peace, an ebullition on which no deep or definite
meaning should be forced. Reading it in this mood,
we should have to underline the word 'rather' in the
first sentence; to ask how Virgil, if he attached
momentous significance to the poem, came to include it in a volume he repeatedly refers to as a
collection of light verse; to stress the fact that we
are still in the woodlands, still surrounded by
the goats and sheep of the rural scene; and to assume

that, when these friendly and familiar beasts surprise us by their apocalyptic behaviour, Virgil is only indulging in one of those playful moments that are so characteristic of his pastoral Muse. At the same time we shall have great difficulty in discounting the strictly factual, if not precise, prophecies and the very concrete conception of a Wonder-child that he has seen fit to introduce into the work. If, as I do, the reader finds it impossible to dismiss these as the mere by-product of a lyrical impulse, we had better pass on to the next interpretation and see how the poem reads as a straightforward political prophecy.

II

Here everything runs smoothly – up to a point. If we begin by asking from what source Virgil derived the peculiar form in which his oracle is cast, we have not far to seek. The idea of cyclical World-Ages was familiar to Graeco-Roman thought, and the doctrine of eternal recurrence,[1] which he enunciates when he says that Achilles must return to Troy, is found in Greek philosophy from the time of Pythagoras[2] to that of the Stoics and beyond. All this was part of Virgil's education. Nor is it difficult to guess where he went for the central idea of a Wonder-child on which he hangs his general theme. When, in the first

1. Pythagoras may have imbibed this doctrine from the Buddhist East. For a modern revival of it, the reader is referred to P. D. Ouspensky's great work, *A New Model of the Universe*.

2. J. Carcopino, in his penetrating study, *Virgile et le Mystère de la IV Eglogue*, finds a source in Pythagoreanism for every concept that Virgil has embodied in his poem.

lines of the poem, he refers us to 'Sibylline song', he has admitted his source.

The so-called Sibylline Books were said to have contained the oracular utterances of a Sibyl or prophetess who operated from Cumae in Southern Italy in the 6th century B.C. – the place and time in which the Pythagorean philosophy developed. The original books had been destroyed before Virgil's birth, but more or less plausible reconstructions of their contents were current in his day. Besides, he was an antiquary, and we have already seen that he knew enough of the books to use them as his authority for predicting the end of the Iron Age. Is it likely, either that his knowledge stopped here, or that the books themselves did not proceed to state that a new Golden Age would follow? If they did so, it is highly probable that they connected the change of era with the birth of a Wonder-child, if only because Virgil enlarges on this part of the theme, and the later imitations[1] of the older books, which we possess in part, do much the same. The poet, then, seized on this striking idea, and by way of complimenting his friend Pollio was bold enough to foretell that the new age would dawn in his consulship. It is true that he does not explicitly state that the Child too will be born in that year, but he suggests it; and the deceptive appearance of precision in the forecast lends weight and content to the

1. At the risk of confusing the reader, I must not disguise the fact that there were many 'Sibyls' in the ancient world, and several sets of Sibylline Oracles, including one of Jewish origin, which Virgil may possibly have known. This 'orientation' of Virgil's prophecy is discussed by W. W. Tarn in the *Journal of Roman Studies*, XXII (1932).

promises which he triumphantly makes to a world that has long been tortured by civil strife.

So far so good; but if we consider Virgil to have deliberately committed himself, if only in his own mind, to the birth of a particular child and to a pair of contemporary parents, our difficulties begin. I will not weary the reader by passing in review and separately dismissing all the baby candidates, born and unborn, who have been nominated for the place of honour. There are grave objections to all of them, including a child of Pollio[1] himself, who do not qualify by being the offspring of one of the two rulers of the Roman world when Virgil wrote, namely Octavian and Antony. The wording of the poem demands that the Child's father shall have pacified the world. Influential as he was, Pollio had scarcely done that. Only Octavian, and perhaps Antony, could be described in such terms. Each of these took a new wife in the year of the poem – Octavian married Scribonia, and Antony married Octavian's sister Octavia. The dates would thus fit in either case, if we allow Virgil to have written rather late in 40 B.C., and do not press him too hard when he anticipates by informing the mother that the ten long months have come to an end. It is true that Antony, as all Rome knew, had for some time been far too much preoccupied with Cleopatra in the East to be a very suitable recipient of such honours from Virgil. But he qualifies, none the less,

1. Carcopino, in the work I have already cited, ingeniously overcomes these objections and elects for a son of Pollio. E. K. Rand (in *The Magical Art of Virgil*, 1931) comes to much the same conclusion.

through his marriage to Octavia.[1] Moreover, the field is narrowed still further in favour of these two great men by another passage in the poem. When Virgil addresses the Child as 'dear offspring of the gods, great increment of Jove', it is hard to believe that he is not thinking of the great Julian line, the family with which they were both connected, and which was officially credited with a divine origin (from Jove through Venus), and already boasted of at least one god, the deified Julius Caesar.

On the whole, then, everything points to Octavian, with Antony as runner-up. But why, if Virgil wished to designate either of these men as the father of the babe, did he not do so? Why are we met with deliberate ambiguity at every point where we attempt to pin him down? For several reasons. First because Virgil is Virgil, and that is his way of writing poetry. Secondly because he did not care to risk the ridicule he might have incurred had the boy-child of his prophecy turned out to be a girl.[2] And lastly because, writing in 40 B.C., he did not know that the long duel between Octavian and Antony was to end in Antony's total eclipse and the establishment of Augustus as undisputed head of the state. He would not have dared to name either of the two for fear of offending the other. He was forced by the circumstances, this time, to 'set a trap for scholars' – a trap

1. Some scholars think we have here a wedding-hymn written for this marriage. It contains echoes from a comparable poem by Catullus; but I do not agree with D. A. Slater (*Classical Review*, XXVI, 1912) in his deduction that Antony and Octavia are the pair.

2. It did, in the case of Octavian and Scribonia. Their daughter, Julia, subsequently so notorious, was born in 39.

we fall into when we ransack the poem for convincing clues. He has hinted that he meant no one in particular, by making it impossible either for his contemporaries or for us to decide whom he meant. And incidentally he succeeded in writing a prophecy which, in spite of its deceptive air of precision, there was no need for him ever to revise or withdraw. Thus, in the end, it seems that the political interpretation of the poem approaches much nearer to the lyrical than might have been expected.

III

But there are some who have been dissatisfied with either reading of the poem, and have been led by its real or superficial resemblances to the style of Old Testament prophecy to suggest that Virgil derived his inspiration from Jewish literature. I myself am more impressed by the differences than by the likeness between Virgil and Isaiah. Nor have we any valid reason other than this probably accidental resemblance for supposing that Virgil had so much as heard Isaiah's name. He was certainly a very learned young man, and well-read in the literature of Alexandria, where the Old Testament was known in its Greek form. We cannot prove that he did not have access to the Septuagint version or that he had not talked with friends in Rome or Naples who knew it. But I think we can say that, if he did come across the Messianic scriptures and feel inspired by them, he decoded their message very badly. Nothing could be less spiritual, in the Biblical sense, than his material, though at the same time idyllic, conception of the Golden Age. And, as we have seen, he had plenty of material at hand to help him make a Roman oracle.

But in saying this I am by no means rejecting the Christian explanation of the poem which we come to now in our survey. The Church, as it gained strength in Rome, was quick to claim Virgil as one of nature's Christians before the time of Christ. When the Emperor Constantine in the 4th century established Christianity as the state religion, he identified the Child of Virgil's prophecy with Christ; and much later Dante made it clear that he regards Virgil as the next best thing to a Christian. But the acceptance of Constantine's view does not oblige us to prove or even to imagine that Virgil had any direct contact with Jewish literature. It asks far more of us than that. It asks us to believe that Virgil had himself been visited by a pre-vision of the birth of Christ and had translated his revelation in terms natural to a poet writing as a Roman some forty years before that momentous event. He had seen through a glass darkly – but he had seen.

Of this theory I will only say that we know too little of the human mind and are still too ignorant of the real nature of time for any wise man to dismiss it as absurd. If we are startled by it into thinking unaccustomed thoughts, so much the better. At all events, the very fact that men so notable and so far apart in time or temperament as St Augustine, Constantine, Dante, and Alexander Pope concur in blessing it, should teach us to impose no limit on the breadth and depth of meaning we may look to find in Virgil's poetry.

I have attempted to hold the scales fairly through a long series of arguments, and I must now give my own conclusions. For me, the three interpretations have merged into one, without losing their individual validity. The Fourth Eclogue is a lyrical rhapsody. It is a Roman oracle too. It is also a vision, conditioned by its date, but influenced none the less by those mysterious forces which, even as Virgil wrote, were gathering strength in Palestine to shape the future of mankind.

DAPHNIS AT HEAVEN'S GATE

'He is a portion of the loveliness
Which once he made more lovely.'
Shelley, *Adonais*

IT would be pleasant to dwell on the charm and
subtleties of the Fifth Eclogue; to point out with
what tact the youthful Mopsus secures the com-
fortable seat he wants, and how handsomely
Menalcas atones for his unhappy reference to Amyntas; or to enlarge on the lyrical beauty of the songs
that emerge from the friendly challenge. For in no
other Eclogue has Virgil given more perfect expression to his feeling of the intimate kinship of man
and beast and rock.

But even though I hope the reader will have
detected these qualities in the poem for himself, I
am pretty sure that the first question he will ask is,
'Who is Daphnis?' We have met him as a handsome
swain in the Second Eclogue; in the Third as a boy
who has had his bow and arrows smashed by
Menalcas (now his worshipper); in the Seventh he
is old enough to preside at a singing-match; and in
the Eighth we see him again, as the recalcitrant lover
whom only witchcraft can induce to abandon the
pleasures of the town. But here he seems to be a god.

The answer is that in this poem Virgil does indeed
kill Daphnis, the ideal country lad and hero of the
Sicilian shepherd fraternity – as Theocritus did
before him. But he goes further and imagines his

enrolment among the minor gods of Olympus as the special patron of the pastoral community whose ornament he had been in life, thus transcending the usual limits of the rather obscure Greek story of Daphnis's life and death. And I can only suggest that he does so because he is a poet, and an original one, who felt it an integral part of his task to write the lovely song of praise he has put into Menalcas's mouth, in which an ideal shepherd, by triumphing over death, establishes for ever the unity of man with the living universe that surrounds him.

For me this is enough. But I know very well that from ancient times to the present day other lovers of Virgil have found very good reasons for thinking that, under the disguise of Daphnis, Virgil is lamenting the recent death of a beloved contemporary. I am not referring to Tenney Frank's theory[1] that this was the poet Cornificius – there is little evidence to support this attractive view; nor to the suggestion that Virgil is mourning for a brother called Flaccus – no sensible poet would think he was doing an obscure relative a service by attempting to promote him to Olympus at one stroke of the pen; but to the more tenable theory that this apotheosis of Daphnis is to be read as the counterpart of the recent official deification of the dictator Julius Caesar.

Unfortunately, to my way of thinking, everything appears at first sight to favour the allegorizers here. It all fits in very neatly. The 'cruel death' suits Caesar's end almost better than that of Daphnis; Caesar (according to Servius) did introduce Bacchic

1. Put forward by him in *Vergil, A Biography* (1922).

rites into Italy; Daphnis's 'lovely flock' is readily identifiable with the Roman people; Daphnis had 'loved Menalcas too', and Caesar had specially favoured Virgil's homeland in Cisalpine Gaul – and so on. The facts that Daphnis died as a lad, and Caesar as an elderly man with a bald head; that Daphnis's mother is alive to mourn him, whereas Caesar's had died many years before her son was assassinated; that 'the good Daphnis stands for peace', whereas Caesar had been fighting for the last sixteen years of his life, and incidentally had cut off the hands of every man who resisted him in Uxellodunum – all these and other trifling incongruities are lightly brushed aside. And indeed, as Professor H. J. Rose says in his *Handbook of Latin Literature*, with Octavian in power it was quite in order for Virgil, or anyone else, to praise his 'father' Julius Caesar to the skies. But this does not prove that Virgil does so here. And we might well ask why, if he was at liberty to laud Caesar openly, he has adopted this baffling camouflage for his admiration.

Let me confess that I am conscious of some prejudice in arguing the case against the allegory. But prejudice is the hardest thing to avoid in literary judgements. And I not only feel this to be a question of good taste, but would go so far as to say that a lovely poem is spoilt for me, when the dead Dictator is dragged on to the stage. My feelings towards Julius Caesar have not been left unaffected by recent events in Europe. However, Virgil was not an Englishman; there is much to show that he did make a hero of Caesar; and I must not allow myself to promote topical reactions to the status of an argument. Let us see whether we have no stouter weapons to rely on.

I spoke just now of good taste. We are dealing with some of the best poetry of a first-rate poet, who may sometimes have written with speed but certainly did not publish in careless haste. His caprice in repeatedly using the same names for different characters in his book must be quite conscious and deliberate.[1] We have already found Daphnis appearing elsewhere in the *Eclogues* in four capacities, none of which tallies very well with his mythological status in the Fifth, still less with his supposed rôle as Julius Caesar – and we cannot complain. It is Virgil's way; and perhaps none of the duplications amounts to absolute incongruity. But a fifth and worse case remains to be examined.

In the year after Julius Caesar's death, Octavian gave a spectacle in his adoptive father's honour. During the games, and in full daylight, we are told that a 'star', which was probably a comet, made its appearance in the sky and was hailed as the soul of Caesar on its way to heaven. In the Ninth Eclogue, Virgil advises a shepherd to adjust his calendar by this newly-risen light, the star of Caesar – and *Daphnis* is that shepherd's name. In fact, if the allegory in the Fifth Eclogue is to stand, Daphnis, alive, is told in the Ninth to watch his own departing soul in its ascent to Olympus. This is worse than

1. A glance at the Glossary will show the reader what I mean. At the same time, I must admit that it has been argued that every name in the *Eclogues* represents one and always the same person. See Léon Herrmann, *Les Masques et les Visages dans les Bucoliques de Virgile* (Brussels, 1930).

incongruous. I find it hard to believe that Virgil was guilty of such inadvertence.

That is my case. But I may be wrong; and I have most of the scholars against me. At all events I shall continue to draw a sharp distinction in my own mind between Daphnis as the darling of the countryside and Daphnis the Conqueror of Gaul.

VI

THE SONG OF SILENUS

'Then, with a shout, we leapt upon him and
flung our arms round his back.'
Homer, Odyssey, IV

THE Sixth Eclogue can be read and enjoyed in an
entirely non-controversial spirit. Yet, apart from its
charm, the poem, which like the Fourth deals with a
somewhat loftier theme than the rest, contains
several points that challenge attention. The dedication itself is one of these. Virgil's choice of his
legendary material is another. And a third (closely
connected with the second) is the curious manner in
which his friend Gallus is suddenly brought into
the picture.

To begin, then, with the introductory lines – we
are not certain who this Varus was. Servius thinks
he was the Publius Alfenus Varus who was entrusted with the allotment of lands to Octavian's
soldiers, and confiscated Virgil's farm – or else did
not. But we have already seen good reason to doubt
the several variations of this tale, and our doubts
are intensified when we read on the same page the
alternative suggestion that he was Publius Quincti-
lius Varus, who, some fifty years *after* this Eclogue
was composed, lost three legions for Augustus in
the depths of Germany. Whoever Varus was, and
whatever the poet's obligation to him may have
been, Virgil disposes of any hopes he may have

entertained of having his achievements sung by his friend, as adroitly as he does for Pollio in the Eighth Eclogue, and even more firmly. The interesting point is that, while thus excusing himself from writing contemporary epic, Virgil gives us a straightforward account, in the first person, of his past and future plans for poetical work. He tells us that he is going to devote himself to rural melodies; the impulse that inspired the *Eclogues* is not yet exhausted, nor are the *Georgics* yet conceived. All there remains for us to ask is who were the kings and what the battles that he once had thought of making his theme. Is this an intimation that he had already imagined an *Aeneid* and rejected the plan, only to resume it in later life; or had some other historical epic for a short time occupied his attention? Tenney Frank thinks he had actually begun the *Aeneid* by the time he wrote this Eclogue, indeed before Julius Caesar's death. But Servius accepts the second explanation and tells us that the young Virgil began a poem about the kings of Alba Longa (the mother-city of Rome), but abandoned the project on account of the harshness of their names – an objection to which the god of poetry had no doubt given due weight before he touched the poet's ear.

Apart from the dedication, the poem itself tells us interesting things about Virgil's inward history. The account of the creation with which Silenus opens his song is a summary of that given by the Epicurean philosopher Lucretius in his great poem *The Nature of the Universe*. Elsewhere Virgil refers more than once to his own early and persistent interest in philosophy, and by repeated references to Lucretius and echoes from his work makes it obvious how much he was indebted to the older poet, though he never mentions him by name.

I myself feel that Virgil's interest in Epicurus is sufficient reason for the prominence he gives in the Eclogue to this piece of Epicurean philosophy. But its inclusion caused Servius (or maybe one of his predecessors) to put forward the theory that, under the alias of Silenus, Virgil is recalling or even parodying the teaching of his tutor Siro, the Epicurean lecturer at whose feet both he and Varus had sat. Tenney Frank for once agrees with him and joins the allegorizers. Yet the more I read the poem, the more alien do I find its mood to the spirit of parody, allegory, or anything but straightforward and transparent poetry. I am quite convinced that we should be wrong in depriving Silenus of his purely mythological status.

Of this, there is not much to be said. Silenus was one of the minor figures of the Greek pantheon, a satyr-like attendant on Dionysus, the god of wine. In this passage at least, he bears a curious resemblance to Proteus, the Old Man of the Sea, whose story as given us by Homer I refer to at the head of this essay. The old reprobate was evidently a consummate artist, and we must look leniently on his morals. But Conington's scruples are not so easily appeased. He takes so sinister a view of the 'reward' Silenus had in mind for Aegle that he omits the whole passage from his translation. Servius, who lived too soon to benefit by the example of Dr Bowdler, takes a very different and even more amusing line. After assisting the dull student by filling in the blank, he commends Virgil's modesty for leaving something unexpressed.

The poet's choice and handling of the tales included in Silenus's repertory have been much discussed and have come under heavy fire from Victorian scholars. I quote only the patronizing and subtly disparaging remark of T. E. Page: 'The Epicurean theory of creation and the myths which follow are merely regarded by Virgil as both affording material for the display of his poetic skill.' Might we not with equal propriety compliment Homer, Dante, and Shakespeare on their adroitness in choosing the themes best adapted to their not inconsiderable talents? Why not give Virgil credit for a genuine interest in his material, whatever caused him to select it, and enjoy the artistry with which he has handled each well-known tale and caught its most picturesque moment in a few masterly words? All I can find to blame him for is the trouble he has put me to in supplementing his brevity for the benefit of such readers as may care to consult my glossary. In one case, indeed, he has made my task impossible, by not even giving us Atalanta's name; and I seize this occasion to explain that she was a swift-footed maiden whose suitors had to beat her in a race or die. In the end she was won by Milanion, who had the forethought to provide himself with three golden apples and throw them at her feet as she outstripped him.

But perhaps there *is* some cause for comment, even for surprise, when, in the midst of this mythological cavalcade, we come upon a living man, the poet

Gallus. Conington finds 'great incongruity' here. Servius, less prone to criticize where he does not understand, suggests indebtedness to Gallus on Virgil's part and once more brings up the old story of the evictions and the confiscated farm. Virgil may perhaps have been indebted to Gallus; but what is far more to the point in explaining this passage is the fact that Gallus was a fellow-poet, that Virgil loved him dearly, and that he wholeheartedly admired his work. It has been thought likely that, if we had Gallus's poems before us and could re-read the Eclogue in their light, all would be clear and the abruptness of his appearance on the stage would be removed. The German scholar F. Skutsch[1] went so far as to argue with great ingenuity and learning that the various episodes covered by Silenus's song form a sort of synopsis of one or more of Gallus's works. It is indeed an attractive thought that some gleams from these lost jewels may filter through to us not only in the last Eclogue but in this one also. Yet it is difficult to believe that Virgil composed a poem consisting for by far the greater part of a mere résumé of the recent work of a living poet; and I myself prefer to seek the clue in the concluding paragraph of the Eclogue, and ask whether Virgil himself is not referring us to his source (just as he does in the Fourth Eclogue), when he tells us that Silenus gave the two lads the same songs as the fortunate Eurotas had once heard from Apollo's lips. If we could discover an earlier Greek poet who had handled this theme at length, I think our quest for Virgil's sources would be at an end. Nor would

1. *Aus Vergils Frühzeit* (1901) and *Gallus und Vergil* (1906).

his use of such material from a Greek poem entail anything to surprise us.

However that may be, I find this undisguised and temporary 'apotheosis' of Gallus much easier to swallow than the alleged apotheosis of Julius Caesar under the alias of Daphnis in the Fifth Eclogue. Moreover, as we shall see when we come to the Tenth, it was not beyond Virgil's whimsical genius to experiment still more boldly with his friend and to picture him in far more embarassing scenes than this.

What *is* intriguing is that this high compliment should have been paid to Gallus in a poem that Virgil dedicates, not without a good measure of conventional flattery, to Varus. However, we know too little of the relationships that obtained between the three men to explain away this apparent anomaly; and Varus's position in the trio remains obscure. But an interesting sidelight is thrown on the literary coterie to which Virgil and Gallus belonged, and of which we get tantalizing glimpses here and there in the *Eclogues*, by a delightful story in Servius, which I should in any case have quoted for its own sake. Of its authenticity I shall say nothing more than that the date of Cicero's death, in 43 B.C., makes it just possible that the tale is as true as it is good.

According to Servius, then, Virgil's recitations of this Eclogue impressed his friends so favourably[1] that they decided to put it on the stage, and it was sung by the actress Cythēris, whom we meet under the name of Lycōris as Gallus's mistress in the last

1. No wonder, if Skutsch is right. Gallus would of course take kindly to so effective an advertisement of his own poetry.

Eclogue. Cicero, attending one of these perform-
ances, was so much captivated[1] that he asked who
had written the words, and on securing an introduction to the young poet, hailed him as 'Rome's
second hope', thereby paying himself as great a
compliment as Virgil.

1. Servius uses the same word, *stupefactus*, as Virgil does in VIII
when describing the mental condition of the lynxes who listened to
the music of Damon and Alphesiboeus.

VII

THE SINGING-MATCH

'I've a grand memory for forgetting.'
R. L. Stevenson

HERE we have another strictly amoebaean contest, like that of the Third Eclogue, except that the singers are given four lines each instead of two in every round. Another and more significant difference is that this time the result is not a dead-heat but a decisive victory for one of the performers. This means that Virgil has once more set himself a delicate task. If the poems he puts into Thyrsis's mouth do not prove inferior to those of Corydon, we shall be left with the feeling that injustice has been done to the loser; while, if they are to be inferior, Virgil must deliberately lower his standard when writing for Thyrsis. It has amused critics to attempt to decide how the poet escapes from this dilemma.

Actually it is very hard to detect any drop in level marked enough to justify the resounding victory that Corydon is allowed to score.[1] The unfortunate Thyrsis is, of course, handicapped from the very start by being given the second place – a severe disadvantage, as I pointed out in my Essay on the Third Eclogue. As a result, less pleasing themes are

1. Professor H. J. Rose is most ingenious in detecting a number of slight blemishes in Thyrsis's style (*The Eclogues of Vergil*, 1942, pp. 145–147).

forced upon him more than once. When Corydon sings of spring, what can Thyrsis do but fall back on the alleviations of winter? Yet he acquits himself well, and I am inclined to think that it is a difference of character between the two shepherd-poets, rather than a contrast between their artistic achievements, that Virgil intends us to detect. In the first round, for instance, Corydon not only combines with modesty a laudable degree of ambition, but shows himself to be a generous friend, whereas Thyrsis alienates our sympathies by an excess of self-confidence. Again, in the second round, Priapus might well take umbrage, not so much at the quantity and quality of his perquisites, as at the mercenary and disrespectful attitude of his devotee. Nor, if he is wise, will the little scarecrow god place much reliance on the promise of a golden statue – that is sheer bombast. Indeed, one feels that in Thyrsis's garden he is lucky to be made of marble, not of wood; and that, if things go wrong with the flock, he will certainly be as roundly blamed as the Wine-god is, in a later quatrain, for the parching of the vines.

However, if this difference in amiability between the two lads is not enough, we may be sure that Virgil, with his usual cunning, has left himself a loophole to escape by. Meliboeus's excellent memory carries him through six rounds of the contest without a hitch, and then fails completely, long before the knock-out blow is delivered by Corydon. If, up to this moment, equal points have been scored, and neither Thyrsis nor Virgil has disgraced himself, it must be afterwards, in the unreported rounds, which we shall never hear, that we must imagine Thyrsis, though putting up a gallant show, to weaken gradually, and to take the final count. In fact, Meliboeus's memory fails because Virgil himself has failed in the attempt to write inferior verse.

Apart from this intriguing puzzle, the only difficulties that the poem presents are minute or imaginary. We have already learnt enough of Virgil's way with geography to feel no surprise when we find a couple of Arcadian lads driving down their flocks to the banks of 'Smooth-sliding Mincius, crowned with vocal reeds'. If taxed on this point, Virgil might well have replied that they were Arcadian in their spirit and accomplishments. It is certainly in this non-geographical sense that the phrase 'Arcadians both' became a catchword with our ancestors, though I am at a loss to explain why and when it assumed its disparaging tone.[1]

Servius, in commenting on the Eclogue, falls once more into an allegorizing mood. We are not only faced with the possibility that Daphnis may be Caesar again, but we are invited to think that Virgil, assuming yet another alias, is Corydon here. From this, it is an easy step to identify the defeated Thyrsis with the Mevius or Bavius whom Virgil has held up to ridicule in the Third Eclogue – we can take our choice. Codrus too becomes a living poet, though a better one, for whom Servius quotes a contemporary sponsor named Valgius.

This is all very well, and indeed, for all we know, there may be references here to the literary coterie I

1. Maybe Byron was responsible, when he wrote: ' "Arcades ambo" *id est* – blackguards both'. *Don Juan*, canto IV, xciii.

have already spoken of. But once one starts allegorizing it is difficult to stop, and Servius carries things to the point of absurdity when he suggests that the Daphnis of this Eclogue is once more the divine being that Virgil makes of him in the Fifth, because it took a god to assure Meliboeus of the safety not only of his wandering billy-goat but of his kids as well. We, bringing our mortal intellect to bear on the problem, find no difficulty in supposing that the kids had followed their runaway senior, as kids do, and that Daphnis had spied the whole party, with Meliboeus in chase not far behind them.

VIII

DAMON AND ALPHESIBOEUS

'Lynxes do not exist in Italy.'
T. E. Page
'One of the least successful of the Eclogues.'
R. C. Trevelyan

THE Eighth Eclogue is prefaced by as elaborate an introduction as the Sixth, but this time it is to Pollio, not to Varus, that Virgil excuses himself for preferring the pastoral to the narrative muse. It is true that he does not mention Pollio by name, as he does when he compliments him so highly in the Fourth; also that Servius for some reason takes it for granted that he means Octavian, not Pollio. But the dates and references fit Pollio best, and it is generally accepted that he is the person meant. Both before and after his consulship in 40 B.C. he was in the north, and in 39 he had been despatched on a punitive expedition against a Dalmatian tribe, and so might aptly be imagined by Virgil as passing the mouth of the River Timavus in Venetia and sailing down the Adriatic Sea on his triumphant return from his mission. Moreover, he is known to have written tragedies, though we do not possess them and cannot tell to what extent they merited the praise which Virgil and Horace[1] bestow on them. The singing-match recorded in the poem itself is not really amoebaean, but more like the friendly exchange of songs that we have had in the Fifth

1. Odes, II. I.

Eclogue. There is no umpire, no decision between the rival performers; both sing of love, but there is no deliberate contrast in their ways of handling the theme; and the two songs do not even correspond exactly in their structure.

Many modern editors are at pains to point out how much Virgil owes to Theocritus throughout the poem and particularly in the second half. They also sprinkle their notes with the word 'artificial', and T. E. Page gives some precision to his use of this ambiguous and maltreated term by such remarks as 'Lynxes do not exist in Italy, but the whole scene is imaginary'; to which the only adequate reply is, 'Exactly so'. I have already tilted, in the Introduction, against these misconceptions of the poet's aims. I could go further and cite Voltaire and Macaulay on the other side. But in questions of taste, especially in deciding where artifice comes in and art goes out, every reader must be his own authority. Those who love Virgil love this poem. For them its 'artificiality' is art. Others may fall back on that useful word to crystallize their disapproval of a thing not fully understood.

A few words on the witchcraft poem. The theme is taken from an Idyl by Theocritus, with many a change, including the happy ending. But it is not these differences between the two poets to which I wish to draw attention, so much as the ubiquity and persistence of magic ceremonial and procedure. What satisfied Greek readers as sound witchcraft in the 3rd century B.C., and Romans in the 1st, would have passed muster in Jacobean England, and scarcely needs a note today. Religions come and go:

magic, for the most part, remains the same. I have verified my impression that to this day there are folk in England who stick pins into effigies[1] of people they dislike. The methods Amaryllis used are only a little more elaborate, and, for all I know, they may yet be in vogue.

Moeris, of course, must have been an exceptionally powerful sorcerer, if Amaryllis does not overstate his claims. As a practising werewolf, he contrasts very oddly with his namesake in the next Eclogue, a disillusioned elderly shepherd who is no match for wolves. As for his further accomplishments, no spiritualist should boggle at the claim that he could call up ghosts from deep down in the grave. And if some sceptic should object that the shifting of a standing crop is an even more formidable undertaking, I should refer him to the excellent Servius, who tells us that such things were actually done. At any rate there was a law against them in the Twelve Tables. Which goes some way to prove the attempt, if not the deed.

When I spoke just now of Amaryllis's magic technique, I begged the question whether two people are involved in this dramatic scene or only one – in addition of course to Daphnis, who arrives just after the curtain has dropped. The usual interpretation (indeed the only one I have seen) is that two are present, the unnamed wife as chief performer, and a servant called Amaryllis, as assistant. But Virgil leaves us quite free to regard the song as a monologue, with Amaryllis addressing admonitions

1. 'Mommets', as they are called, owing, originally, to a false idea that idols of Mahomet were made by his followers.

to herself. I feel that this interpretation heightens the effect.

It has also been disputed whether Damon, when singing his song, leans against the trunk of an olive-tree or on a staff of olive-wood – Virgil merely says 'a smooth olive'. Much has been written in this connexion about the gnarled and rugged habit of the olive-tree, and of the discomfort of leaning against it. Much could also be said about the difficulty of playing a pipe with one hand otherwise occupied. I prefer to leave Damon with both hands free for his instrument, and to think that, if olive-trunks are mostly rough, that is the reason why Virgil took the trouble to tell us that Damon chose a smooth one for his back. His thought for the comfort of the shepherd is as characteristic as his concern for the satisfaction of the flock. It is Virgil at his best to take the sheep's view of the beauty of the morning dew on the grass.

To conclude, Servius, as usual, has a good story to tell us. It concerns Cicero once more; in fact it is taken from the poem he wrote in honour of his own achievements as consul in the year 63 B.C. His wife had just sacrificed and was about to pour a drink-offering on the ashes, when these burst into flame, just as they did for Amaryllis. This meant – it is not stated why – that Cicero would be elected consul in the same year. And he was.

IX

THE ROAD TO TOWN

Two countrymen meet on the way to town and fall into conversation. One of them, Moeris, has just been evicted from his holding to make place for a veteran – we have come upon a comparable scene in the First Eclogue. His companion, Lycidas, who is behind-hand with the news, recalls the endeavour of a fellow-farmer, Menalcas, who is something of a poet, to save the district from this legalized brigandage by a petition in verse to the authorities. But Moeris is able to inform him of the failure of this move, and dwells on the dangers that Menalcas underwent in his attempt. The pair then while away the time by reciting such verses as they can remember from the poems of their friend.

This sounds simple, and read in this way, which is the way I recommend to the English reader, the poem *is* simple, as well as delightful. Unfortunately, the topical allusions it contains are so suggestively precise, and yet, when scrutinized, so vague, as to leave room for a flood of speculation. Moreover, the poem bears certain affinities to an Idyl of the Greek pastoral poet Theocritus which has been shown to bristle with camouflaged references to real people; and, although it is always dangerous to argue from Theocritus to Virgil, since Virgil is nowhere more original than in his 'imitations', the net result is that we are faced once more, and in an even acuter form, with the questions already touched on in discussing the First Eclogue: 'Does Virgil mean us to take the poet Menalcas for himself, and is it his own farm and the loss of it that he is deploring?'

Let me assure the reader at once that I am not going to take him far, this time, down the labyrinthine ways of hypothesis, allegory, and reconstruction. My feeling is that if Virgil set out to make the poem autobiographical (which I do not believe), he for some reason so obscured the clues as to defeat his purpose, possibly because he still felt himself on dangerous ground, but still more probably because the instincts of a poet overruled the first intentions of a reporter. All we are left to say is that the poem seems too factual to pass as completely imaginary, and that Menalcas may well stand for some actual farmer-poet who made an appeal to Varus, one of the commissioners, when the lands of Cremona had been seized and those of its neighbour Mantua were threatened. But the identification of Menalcas with Virgil is not proven (in spite of his last speech in the Fifth Eclogue): there is nothing to compel us to the belief that Virgil devoted a whole eclogue to the praise of his own poetry.

I am not denying that those who accept the identification, and chase the elusive clues, put themselves in the way of some excellent sport. Indeed the hunt becomes exciting at as early a point as Lycidas's second speech, where, if Menalcas is Virgil, we may well feel that we are listening to the poet's description of his own ancestral farm. Scholars have even visited the locality in the hope of identifying the spot. No excursion could be more enjoyable. But the reports they bring back are unconvincing – as anyone who has studied the poet's evasive technique might have foretold. Moreover, as T. E. Page and E. K. Rand have pointed out, Lycidas is surely describing a district, not a single farm.[1]

In the snatches of song that Virgil causes the two friends to quote from Menalcas's works, we certainly seem to be offered clues, but the scent of the red herring is strong in the air. These lines are not quotations from the other Eclogues. If they are Virgil's (and they sound like his) he either wrote them for insertion in this work or has taken them from poems of his own that he did not include for publication in his final selection. Actually he has left us quite free to regard them as extracts from the work of a fellow-poet – one of the 'singing-swans' of Mantua, perhaps – whom he disguises under the Greek name of Menalcas. But I do not stress that possibility so much as the care that Virgil used, if he did write the verses himself, to prevent his 'Menalcas' from being caught in the act of quoting Virgil and so enabling us to clinch the identification of the two. He has even gone to the trouble, in the first quotation, of making Menalcas give orders to Tityrus (that useful factotum who seems always at hand to look after other people's goats), in spite of the fact that in the Sixth Eclogue he identifies Tityrus with himself. If some case-hardened allegorizer insists, nevertheless, on making Virgil say, 'Feed my goats, Virgil, while I am gone' – my sympathies go out to the goats.

---

1. An interesting discussion of the problem is given by R. S. Conway in *The Vergilian Age* (1928), to which reference has already been made in the Essay on I (p. 127).

The three lines addressed to Varus throw no light on the problem of Menalcas's identity. If a poetical appeal *was* made, we are left to guess who made it, as well as what effect it had. The allusion to the unfinished state of the poem even suggests the possibility that this very Eclogue is itself the famous appeal and the only one that was ever penned.

But there is a point at which conjecture becomes futile; and with the third quotation we happily pass from controversial ground. The Galatea here addressed defeats all attempts to convert her into anyone but her delightful self. It is only to be observed that she is not the country wench who had jilted Tityrus in the First Eclogue, but a sea-nymph whom the Cyclops Polyphemus loved.

The fourth song is equally clear of complexities. It is an undisguised tribute to the deified Julius Caesar. I gave some account of the celestial phenomenon that Virgil recalls, when I cited these lines in my essay on the Fifth Eclogue as evidence against the allegorical interpretation of that poem. Servius rounds off the tale by telling us that Octavian had a golden star placed above the head of his adoptive father when he erected a statue of him in the Capitol.

In the dialogue of the poem there is one point that may strike the reader as odd. I refer to the sudden appearance of two 'real' poets, Cinna and Varius, and the praise that Virgil causes Moeris to bestow on them. We know something of these men, and Virgil's contemporaries knew more. One of them, Cinna, a great friend of the poet Catullus, had been killed in mistake for a namesake while walking in Caesar's funeral procession. The other, Varius, lived to become one of Virgil's literary executors. Here they stand out undisguised, like islands in the misty seas of camouflaged allusion. I take this as a pretty strong hint that when Virgil wants to talk openly about someone he does so, and that for the rest, his allusions to living people, if any, are made deliberately unintelligible, except, maybe, to the literary circle of which he was a member.

I have after all got myself so deeply involved in the intriguing speculations to which the poem invites us that I have left its praises unsung. I see that Servius too is so much preoccupied with the task of reconstructing history from fiction, that he has little space left for his usual titbits of information and enlightenment. He does tell us, however, how Moeris came to lose his voice. It is one of the things that happen to a man when the wolves spy him before he spies the wolves. 'Even the physicians,' he says, 'confirm the truth of this.'

X

GALLUS

'Who would not sing for *Lycidas*? he knew
Himself to sing, and build the lofty rhyme.'
Milton

'What would we not barter of all the epics of the
Empire for a few pages written by Gallus?'
Tenney Frank

No one whom Virgil loved as he loved Gallus
could fail to attract us. And Gallus has other claims
than these on our affection. Here, briefly, is what we
know about this remarkable man.

Gaius Cornelius Gallus was born at Forum Julii
(now Fréjus) in Southern Gaul a year or so after
Virgil. His parents were humble folk, but it would
be wrong to assume that they were Gauls on
account of the name – it was one that several distinguished Romans had already borne. However,
those who know Fréjus and the neighbouring
mountains of the Esterel on the Riviera are free to
interpret his character in whatever terms of early
Celtic influence they may care to imagine.

He must have come to Rome while still a lad, for
we are told that he had published a volume of poems
by the time he was twenty. He seems to have
attracted Julius Caesar's attention and is reported to
have studied philosophy with Virgil under Siro.
But, unlike Virgil, he had political, as well as literary,
ambitions, and, by the time we meet him in the
Eclogues, he had become a trusted lieutenant of
Octavian and had been appointed one of the Com-

missioners for the redistribution of lands in Northern Italy.

The poems of Gallus that Virgil refers to as having been composed in 'Chalcidic verse' were imitations of Greek originals by the Alexandrine poet Euphorion, of Chalcis in Euboea. There is good reason for thinking that these were not identical with the four books of love poems that Gallus is known to have dedicated to his mistress Lycōris. It seems clear, at all events, that it was Gallus's intimate and self-revealing treatment of the theme of love which placed him among the foremost Roman elegists, inspired the regretful admiration of Propertius after his death, and caused Ovid to say that he and his Lycōris would be read from the rising to the setting sun.

But Gallus does not appear to have followed up this early literary success. The soldier and statesman in him overcame the poet, and when next he gave rein to his exuberant fancy, it was in another direction and with tragic results.

He continued for many years to serve Octavian with distinction. At the decisive battle of Actium in 31 B.C., when the fleet of Antony and Cleopatra was routed, Gallus held a high command. He was entrusted with the pursuit to Egypt and played a gallant part in the final operations in that country. The historian Dio Cassius gives us interesting details, which show us that the passionate lover could also be a resourceful and imaginative commander in the field. Gallus captured a town called Paraetonium, on the coast west of Alexandria. When Antony came up to the attack, Gallus was perturbed by the knowledge that he had in his garrison a number of men who had served with Antony and might be won over by him if he were given an opportunity of suborning their loyalty. Gallus let Antony come right up to the walls, and then, as he prepared to address the defenders, he ordered all his trumpeters to sound their instruments together, and to continue the uproar, with the result that Antony was forced to retire without having been able to get a word across.

An assault was made, but it failed, and a naval force was now detailed to attack the place, which had a harbour with a very narrow entrance. Gallus drew chains across this, but left them lying on the bottom, and avoided the appearance of guarding the spot. Antony's fleet incautiously seized the opportunity to sail in during the night. Gallus raised the chains behind them by mechanical means, and, once he had them confined in the harbour, destroyed them easily.

In recognition of his services he was now made the first Prefect or, as we should say, Viceroy of Egypt by Octavian and distinguished himself by quelling a rebellion at Thebes. But power had gone to his head and affected his judgement. Instead of attributing his successes to the Emperor, as tact and policy demanded, he claimed the merit for himself, had his own statues erected everywhere, and even caused self-laudatory inscriptions to be put on the Pyramids. He had enemies enough to ensure that such conduct should be reported at Rome and interpreted as evidence of disloyalty. The matter was dealt with in the Senate, Gallus was recalled, and, though not condemned to death by his old friend Augustus, felt that he had fallen beyond redemption, and took his own life.[1]

Even his poems seem to have suffered from his disgrace, and Ovid's prophecy was not fulfilled. There are few references to them later than those I have mentioned. Quintilian, writing a century after his death, knows his works, and Servius appears to know them. After that they are swallowed up in the dark night that closed down on so much that was beautiful in Greek and Roman letters. Even references to Gallus appear to have been discouraged. The Fourth Book of Virgil's *Georgics*, as first composed, is said by Servius[2] to have contained a long story of which Gallus was the hero. His disgrace and death intervened, Augustus objected, and Virgil substituted for the offending passage the beautiful tale of Orpheus and his Eurydice with which the book now closes.

One more misfortune overtook the ill-starred Gallus, and that, when he had lain for eighteen centuries in the grave. A German named Becker, setting out to write an informative book on how the Romans lived, made him the clothes-peg of his tale. Many a Victorian schoolboy on a prize-giving day has walked up to the platform in unsuspecting innocence and come away with Becker's *Gallus* on his hands.

1. Suetonius, in his *Life of Augustus*, reports that the Emperor complained, with tears, that he was the only man who could not set what limits he chose to his anger with his friends.

2. His statements are dismissed as nonsense by Professor W. B. Anderson (*Classical Quarterly*, xxvii, 1933) and Professor H. J. Rose (*Handbook of Latin Literature*, 1936).

Such was the man whom Virgil has immortalized as the first discarded lover to think of big game as an antidote to love. It was a bold experiment to put him in among the sheep and goats and make a lovelorn swain out of the militant statesman of the Civil Wars, though perhaps no bolder than Milton's when he relieved his sorrow for the death of an under-graduate friend by calling on Arcadia for its tears. Scarcely a commentator till we come to Tenney Frank has resisted the lure of the easy label 'artificial', and, though some have conceded the extraordinary beauty of the poem, Conington, unconquered to the end, complains that 'the identification of shepherd and poet is so rudely managed as to amount to absolute confusion'. Now I will not anticipate the reader's judgement nor spoil his pleasure by dwelling on the subtlety and elegance of this tribute from one poet to another. But there is one clue to its interpretation that all who read the poem should possess. Conington had it before him, in his own words, had he but seen it. For 'the identification of shepherd and poet' had already been made, before Virgil made it, by Gallus himself, in his Lycōris Elegies.

We owe it to Servius that we can reconstruct the story. He tells us that many of the words that Virgil puts into the mouth of Gallus the shepherd are actually quotations from the works of Gallus the poet. If Gallus then, on some real or imaginary campaign or on leave in Greece, had heard that his darling had run off with another officer and had published his grief in pastoral vein, what could be more natural than for his friend Virgil to condole with him in the same idiom? I will even suggest that Gallus in one of his other poems had gently twitted Virgil by picturing him among his sheep and goats, and that this Eclogue is Virgil's reply, full of the playful tenderness that made him dear to all his friends.

If this is really so, if half the words and sentiments of this delightful poem are originally those of Gallus, let us thank Virgil for preserving them for us, yet with such tact and skill that no dismemberment or crude analysis can rob the whole of its unity or make us feel that we are reading anything but a masterpiece of Virgil's own. I like to think that it really was the future Viceroy of Egypt who in the pangs of ill-requited love had had the grace to spare an anxious thought for the dainty feet of his beloved runaway.

GLOSSARY

of legendary, fictional and historical characters and of place-names mentioned in the translation

ACHILLES (IV). The most famous of the Greek captains who took part in the Trojan War; the hero of Homer's *Iliad*. For the significance of Virgil's prophecy about him in IV, see the Essay on that Eclogue.

ADONIS (X). In Greek story Adonis was a beautiful youth fatally loved by Aphrodite, whose outraged husband, Ares, took the form of a wild-boar and killed him. Virgil is here referring to the fact that he was brought up in pastoral surroundings by the Nymphs.

Aphrodite's grief was so great that she secured from Hades permission for Adonis to spend part of each year with her in the upper world. The original cult had reference to the seasonal death and rebirth of vegetation, and one of its special features was the 'Gardens of Adonis', in which flowers were grown round his image. Shakespeare tells part of his tale in *Venus and Adonis*, and a 'Garden of Adonis' figures in Spenser's *Faery Queen* and elsewhere in Elizabethan literature.

AEGLE (VI). A Nymph to whom Virgil attributes a prominent part in the attack on Silenus in VI. The name means 'brilliance' and is thus appropriate to a Naiad or water-sprite.

AEGON (II, V). In II, Aegon is referred to as a sheep-owner and as Menalcas's rival for Neaera's love. In V, however (where he is described as a native of Crete), Menalcas counts on him for a song at the Festival of Daphnis.

AGANIPPE (X). A Naiad, whose spring was situated at the foot of Mt Helicon in the part of Boeotia known as Aonia, and was thus connected with the Muses and poetry.

ALCIMEDON (III). A wood-carver otherwise unknown to us.

ALCIPPE (VII). A farm-girl.

ALCON (V). Here, probably, only a pastoral character, and not the famous archer who accompanied Hercules.

ALEXIS (II, VII). A beautiful lad, loved in II by Corydon and again referred to by him in VII. Suetonius would have us believe that, under the pseudonym of Alexis, Virgil is referring to a friend of his own called Alexander.

ALPHESIBOEUS (V, VIII). Referred to as a champion dancer in V, he sings the witchcraft song in VIII, in competition with Damon.

ALPINE (X). The Alps had no romantic appeal for the Romans. When Gallus feels 'the call of the wild', as he does in X, his thoughts turn to the lower altitudes and milder asperities of Arcadia.

AMARYLLIS (I, II, VIII, IX). In I a country lass in love with Tityrus; in II the rather difficult lady whom Corydon once loved. In the witchcraft song in VIII she lures home her lover, or her husband, Daphnis, by means of magic ritual; and in IX she appears as a general favourite.

AMPHION (II). A mythical hero. In the *Odyssey* (Book XI) he and his brother Zethus are described as the founders of Thebes of the Seven Gates, but Homer does not go on to tell us that when building its walls Amphion played the lyre so beautifully that the stones moved into place of their own accord. Virgil is referring to an earlier stage in the life of this remarkable musician, when he was brought up by shepherds in the mountains of Boeotia.

AMYNTAS (II, III, V, X). A shepherd, mentioned in II as a devotee of the reed-pipe, and in III as a youth dear to Menalcas, who nevertheless, in V, speaks disparagingly of his performance as a musician. In X, Gallus mentions him as a typical country lad, handsome though dark.

ANTIGENES (V). Is referred to by Mopsus as a good-looking boy. There is no reason to identify him (as Servius does) with one of Virgil's friends.

AONIAN (VI, X). Aonia was a part of Boeotia in which Mt Helicon and the Spring of Aganippe were situated. Thus it was connected with the Muses.

APOLLO. See under *Phoebus Apollo*.

ARACYNTHUS (II). A mountain on the borders of Attica and Boeotia.

ARCADY (IV, VII, X). Arcadia was a mountainous country in the centre of the Peloponnesus, or southern peninsula of Greece. Its idealization by Virgil and subsequent poets has some basis in fact. Its hill-pastures and hunting-grounds supported a mainly rural community; it was the original home of the worship of Pan, the shepherds' god, and it remained the chief centre of his cult and of the pastoral music of which he was regarded as the inventor and patron.

ARETHUSA (X). The Nymph Arethusa is invoked by Virgil as a patroness of Sicilian pastoral poetry, though she began her career on the Greek mainland. The story is that, to escape her too ardent lover, the river-god Alpheus, she was turned into a fountain, which flowed under the Ionian Sea and reappeared as a spring in the island of Ortygia, at Syracuse, on the Sicilian coast. Shelley's poetry and the classical accomplishments of those responsible for the christening of H.M. warships have combined to keep her memory green.

ARGO (IV). The famous ship in which a picked band of adventurers (the Argonauts) were reputed to have set out in search of the Golden Fleece. The earliest mention of her is in Homer's *Odyssey*, Book XII, l. 70, where she is referred to as an already famous ship. The full story is told by Apollonius of Rhodes in his epic, the *Argonautica*.

ARION (VIII). The celebrated poet and player of the lyre. We are told that, on a voyage from Sicily to Corinth, he was attacked by the covetous crew for his wealth. Obtaining their leave to play one last piece before his death, he climbed to the bow of the ship and so charmed the gods and the music-loving dolphins by his song that when he leapt into the water the sea-beasts rallied to the rescue and carried him safely to land. Arion is a historical person, who lived about 600 B.C.

ARMENIAN (V). The reference to tigers as Armenian is not merely ornamental, for Bacchus and his cult were connected with the East. See also under *Bacchus*.

ASCRA (VI). A town in Boeotia where the Greek poet Hesiod lived.

ASSYRIA (III, IV). The name was used loosely for the country watered by the Rivers Euphrates and Tigris.

BACCHUS (V, VII). Greek god (also known as Dionysus) concerned with the fertility of vegetation, in particular of the vine, and worshipped with orgiastic rites. His origin is obscure. Homer tells us very little about him, but one passage in the *Iliad* (VI, 130 ff.) certainly connects him with Thrace. In V Daphnis is credited with the distinction of having introduced his cult to the pastoral community.

BAVIUS (III). A contemporary poet who had shown himself hostile to Virgil.

BIANOR (IX). Servius tells us that Bianor was the founder of Mantua.

BRITONS (I). For Virgil's opinion of Britain and the Britons see the Essay on I.

CAESAR (IX). Caius Julius Caesar, the great Dictator,

assassinated in 44 B.C. He is mentioned by name in IX only, but many scholars think that, under the disguise of Daphnis, Virgil is referring in V to his deification. See the Essay on that Eclogue.

CALLIOPE (IV). One of the Nine Muses, whose province was epic poetry. The legendary poet Orpheus was the son of Oeagrus and Calliope.

CERES (V). An Italian goddess of agriculture who was identified with the Greek Demeter. Her connexion with corn led to the poetical use of her name for bread. Hence our 'cereal'.

CHALCIDIC (X). By 'Chalcidic verse' Virgil means poetry written in imitation, or in the style, of the Greek poet Euphorion of Chalcis, in Euboea. See Essay on X.

CHIAN (V). The Aegean island of Chios was noted for its wines.

CHROMIS (VI). A shepherd mentioned only in VI, where he takes part in the assault on Silenus.

CINNA (IX). Gaius Helvius Cinna, the author of an epic poem called *Smyrna*, which was admired by his friend Catullus and evidently by Virgil too. It has not survived. This is the 'Cinna the poet' of Shakespeare's *Julius Caesar*, III, 3 (see Essay on IX).

CIRCE (VIII). The witch encountered by Odysseus, as related in the tenth book of Homer's *Odyssey*.

CODRUS (V, VII). Figures in the title of a song in V, from which we can infer that he was of a quarrelsome disposition. In VII his poetry is highly praised by Corydon, and some scholars, including Servius, think that Virgil is referring to a contemporary poet.

CONON (III). A celebrated Greek mathematician and astronomer of the 3rd century B.C. The other scientist referred to but not named in the same passage in III is possibly Eudoxus, a pupil of Plato.

CORSICAN (IX). Corsican honey was noted for its

bitterness; yews were considered bad for bees; and Virgil supposes yews to have been common in Corsica. Unless we have missed the point, the logic does not appear to be impeccable.

CORYDON (II, VII). A young shepherd. In II, of which he is the subject, he is in a subordinate position, Alexis being 'his master's' favourite. His claim to possess a thousand ewes must be taken as a boastful quotation from the Cyclops' song to Galatea in Theocritus (see H. J. Rose: *The Eclogues of Vergil*, Sather Classical Lectures, 1942; pp. 35–6). In VII he is the victor in a singing-match with Thyrsis.

CREMONA (IX). A town in Northern Italy founded as a Roman colony in 219 B.C. In the Civil Wars it sided against Octavian, who subsequently seized its lands for distribution among his veterans. It was not far from Mantua (Virgil's home town), which only partially escaped the same fate. See Essays on I and IX.

CRETAN (V, X). Crete was famous for its archery. In V we must presume Aegon to have been an immigrant from the island.

DAMOETAS (II, III, V). A countryman mentioned in II as having bequeathed his reed-pipe to Corydon on his deathbed. In III he is very much alive; he is the hired shepherd who, after an exchange of abuse, challenges Menalcas to a singing-match. Nevertheless, in V, we find Menalcas counting on him for a song at the Festival of Daphnis.

DAMON (III, VIII). In III he is referred to as a goat-owner who employs Tityrus and is defeated in a singing-match by Damoetas. In VIII he sings a love-song in competition with Alphesiboeus.

DAPHNIS (II, III, V, VII, VIII, IX). In II Daphnis is a good-looking country lad; in III he is a mere boy, who is bullied by Menalcas; but he figures in V as a deified hero (see Essay on that Eclogue). In VII he reappears as a shepherd who presides at a singing-match. In the witchcraft song in VIII he is the recalcitrant lover whom Amaryllis draws home from town by means of magic spells; and in IX he is a farmer who receives a piece of astronomical advice.

DELIAN (VII). Of Delos, a small island in the Aegean Sea, famous and sacred as the birthplace of Apollo and his sister, Artemis, or Diana.

DODONA (IX). A place in Epirus celebrated for its oracle of Zeus. The god's utterances were detected in the whispering of the leaves in a grove of sacred oaks (see Homer's *Odyssey*, XIV, 327–8).

ETHIOPIAN (X). Virgil mentions Ethiopia as a typically hot country. It was one of the southernmost lands known to the Romans.

EUROTAS (VI). A river of Southern Greece, which rises in Arcadia and flows through Lacedaemon. Virgil is no doubt thinking of Apollo's love for the youth Hyacinthus, whom he courted on its banks.

FAUNS (V, VI). The Italian country-god Faunus was identified in literature with the Greek god Pan. His associate 'Fauns' thus became equivalent to the Satyrs who attended Pan.

GALATEA (I, III, VII, IX). In I she is a country girl who has discarded Tityrus. In III she is described affectionately as a saucy wench by Damoetas. In VII Corydon addresses her in a love-song as the daughter of Nereus, a sea-god – a promotion which shows that Virgil is thinking of her here as the legendary Galatea whom the Cyclops Polyphemus loved. This is certainly true in IX, where the little song addressed to her is derived from the famous and much longer appeal to his sea-love which Theocritus puts into Polyphemus' mouth.

GALLUS (VI, X). Gaius Cornelius Gallus, the poet and friend of Virgil. See the Essays on VI and X.

GARDENS OF THE WEST (VI). Trees bearing golden apples were a wedding present given by Earth to Zeus and Here. *Hesperides* is the name given both to the remote western islands where they grew and to the Nymphs who guarded them. It was with the help of these apples that Milanion succeeded in capturing the swift-footed maiden Atalanta (see Essay on VI).

GRYNEAN WOOD (VI). Grynium was a town on the coast of Asia Minor celebrated for a grove consecrated to Apollo, who had killed a serpent there. The point of the reference in VI is that the story was told by Euphorion of Chalcis, whose poems Gallus imitated (see Essay on X).

HEBRUS (X). The principal river of Thrace.

HERCULES (VII). The Latin name of Heracles, the hero of the Twelve Labours.

HESPER (X). Hesperus, the evening star.

HYBLAEAN (I, VII). Hybla was a town on the slopes of Mt Etna in Sicily, famous for its honey. Virgil's use of the adjective does not imply that he imagined Tityrus to have imported his bees or to take his naps on Etna. He uses it as a literary epithet in I, much as he uses it in VII of the wild-thyme which the bees of Hybla loved.

HYLAS (VI). A lad loved by Heracles, whom he accompanied in the ship *Argo* as far as the coast of Mysia. Landing there with the crew to find fresh water for the voyage, Hylas became separated from his friends. As he gazed down into a spring, the Naiads fell in love with his beauty and dragged him down into the water. The story is told by Apollonius of Rhodes in his *Argonautica* and by Theocritus.

HYLAX (VIII). The name of a watch-dog. It is Greek for 'barker'.

ILLYRIAN SEA (VIII). That part of the Adriatic which washes the shores of Dalmatia.

IOLLAS (II, III). A farmer, who in II may be presumed to be the master of Alexis, and in III is mentioned as one of the lovers of Phyllis.

ISMARUS (VI). A mountain in Thrace, the country of the Orpheus legend. The town of Ismarus is mentioned by Odysseus in the ninth book of the *Odyssey* as the scene of his encounter with the Cicones.

JOVE (III, IV). The supreme Olympian god (the Greek Zeus). The Latin nominative is Iuppiter, genitive Iovis; hence the English names, Jupiter and Jove.

LIBETHRUM (VII). A Thracian town near Mt Olympus. The district was sacred to the Muses.

LINUS (IV, VI). A legendary poet and singer, the son of Apollo, who was reputed, like Orpheus, to have caused the trees to move after him for love of his music.

LUCINA (IV). The goddess of childbirth, equated sometimes with Juno, but here with Diana, the sister of Phoebus Apollo.

LYCAEUS (X). A mountain in Arcadia, one of the centres of the cult of Pan.

LYCIDAS (VII, IX). In VII he is a handsome country lad admired by Thyrsis; in IX a shepherd-poet whom some scholars wish to identify with a member of Virgil's literary circle.

LYCŌRIS (X). The pseudonym used by Virgil for Gallus's mistress, the actress Cythēris, and by Gallus himself in the poems he addressed to his love (see Essays on VI and X). The name and the pseudonym have, as usual, the same scansion.

MACEDONIAN (X). Virgil uses here the more localized term 'Sithonian'. Sithonia was the central peninsula of the three which jut out from Chalcidice in Macedonia.

MAENALUS (VIII, X). A mountain-range in Arcadia sacred to Pan.

MANTUA (IX). A small town standing on an island in
the River Mincius, a tributary of the Po, in Northern
Italy. It was the nearest market-town to the place of
Virgil's birth. The fate of its territories under Octavian and his Commissioners is discussed in the Essays
on I and IX.

MELIBOEUS (I, II, VII). In I a dispossessed farmer
driven into exile. In II, if the same person is meant, he
is still in possession of his flocks. He reappears in VII
as the narrator of the singing-match at which Daphnis
presides.

MENALCAS (II, III, V, IX, X). A countryman. In II he
is the dusky but attractive youth with whom Corydon
contrasts his favourite Alexis. In III he takes on
Damoetas in a singing-match. In V he sings of the
apotheosis of Daphnis and incidentally claims to have
composed II and III, or rather to have learnt them
from the pipe which he presents to Mopsus. Even so,
I do not think Virgil identifies Menalcas with himself,
either in V or in IX, where he figures as a farmer-poet
who has lost his land. In X, he reappears as one of the
rustic swains who rally to the lovelorn Gallus, and
cannot be the poet himself.

MEVIUS (III). A poet contemporary with Virgil, whose
work he criticized unfavourably. Virgil retorts in III,
and Horace called him 'stinking Mevius'. His poetry
has not survived.

MICON (III, VII). A vineyard owner and a hunter.

MINCIUS (VII). The modern Mincio, a tributary of the
River Po in Northern Italy. It flowed past Mantua,
through Virgil's home country.

MNASYLLUS (VI). A shepherd mentioned only in VI,
where he is associated with Chromis in the assault on
Silenus.

MOERIS (VIII, IX). In the witchcraft song in VIII,
Moeris is the champion wizard who supplies Amaryllis

with her herbs and whose prowess in sorcery she handsomely acknowledges. But in IX he has turned into an elderly countryman who has lost his voice and forgotten most of the songs he used to sing as a boy.

MOPSUS (V, VIII). A young shepherd of peculiar tact and charm, who exchanges song about Daphnis with Menalcas in V. In Damon's songs in VIII, he is the future husband of the faithless Nysa.

MUSES (III, IV, VI–X). The Nine Muses, the 'choir of Phoebus', as Virgil calls them in VI, were the goddesses of poetry, music, and literary composition in general. They are invoked or referred to in almost every Eclogue, sometimes as a body (Pierian Maidens, Nymphs of Libethrum, etc.), sometimes individually, as when Thalia is mentioned in VI, and Calliope in IV.

But as used by the Romans and ourselves, the word 'Muse' often means little more than poetry in general, or the poems or style of a particular author (e.g. 'my Muse' in III, and 'the Muse of Sophocles' in VIII). The 'Muses of Sicily' appealed to in IV are not another band of goddesses but a personification of the impulse that had inspired the pastoral poetry of Theocritus.

NAIADS (II, VI, X). Nymphs of fresh water (see under *Nymphs*). In X Virgil addresses them (perhaps because he has begun by invoking the fountain-nymph Arethusa) as though they were Muses, and complains of their indifference to the love-troubles of his friend, the poet Gallus. But it is quite likely that the Muses were themselves originally water-spirits.

NISUS (VI). See under *Scylla*.

NYMPHS (I, II, III, V, VI, VII, IX, X). 'Nymphs' is the general term for the personifications by which the fancy, or the perception, of the Greeks expressed the realities that they sensed in the phenomena of the countryside. The seas, the caves, the trees, the springs, and lakes and rivers, all had their special kinds of Nymphs, of whom Virgil, in the *Eclogues*, mentions only the Naiads, or fresh-water spirits (II and VI), and the Dryads and Hamadryads, who lived in the trees (V and X).

It can be debated whether, to the average educated Roman, the Nymphs amounted to much more than a pretty conceit; but I argue in the Introduction that Virgil made a poet's use of the belief to embody a very genuine apprehension of reality.

NYSA (VIII). The faithless girl who jilts her lover to marry Mopsus in the song of Damon.

ODYSSEUS (VI, VIII). The wandering hero of Homer's *Odyssey* (Virgil uses the Latin name Ulysses, which is no longer favoured in English). The reference in VI is to Odysseus's disastrous passage between the rocky haunt of the monstrous Scylla and the whirlpool of Charybdis (*Odyssey* XII); and in VIII to the transformation of his men into swine by the witch Circe (*Odyssey* X).

ORPHEUS (III, IV, VI, VIII). In Greek story, Thracian Orpheus figures as an early pre-Homeric poet and musician of fabulous skill. Son of the Muse Calliope, he sang so divinely to the harp that even trees and rocks were bewitched and followed him. In VI he is pictured as delighting the Thracian wilds with his music.

In post-Homeric times he was the centre of a number of mystical cults.

OXUS (I). An Asian river flowing into the Aral Sea.

PALAEMON (III). A countryman who judges the singing-match in III.

PALES (V). An Italian goddess (not taken over from Greek mythology), who presided over agricultural life.

PALLAS (II). Pallas Athene (the Roman Minerva) was not only the goddess of wisdom but the patroness of fortified cities, and of Athens in particular.

PAN (II, IV, V, VIII, X). The god of Arcadia, the patron of shepherds, protector of sheep, and inventor of the reed-pipe. His annoyance at finding unemployment among the reeds is described in VIII. In art he is depicted with horns on his forehead and the hind-legs of a goat. He figures thus on the famous Neptune Plate recently dug up at Mildenhall. In X Virgil pictures him, as he had seen his images, with face and brow stained red. This was a common practice – it is referred to in the description of the attack on Silenus in VI.

PARIS (II). The son of Priam, King of Troy, whose seduction of Helen, wife of Menelaus, led to the Trojan War. Virgil is thinking of his youth: he was brought up by the shepherds on Mt Ida.

PARNASSUS (VI, X). A mountain near Delphi in Greece, celebrated as one of the favourite haunts of Apollo and the Muses.

PARTHENIUS (X). A mountain in Arcadia, named, according to Servius, after the virgins who made it their hunting-ground.

PARTHIANS (I, X). The Parthians were successors to the Persian power in Mesopotamia and were for long Rome's most formidable enemies in the East. Their archers were famous, particularly for their skill in shooting behind them as they retreated – hence our 'Parthian shot'.

PASIPHAË (VI). The wife of Minos, King of Crete. The lady was indeed ill-starred. To punish her husband for a broken vow, the gods caused her to fall in love with a beautiful bull. The issue of this unhappy union was the Minotaur, a monstrous creature which was kept in the Labyrinth at Cnossus, till it was killed by

Theseus, with the aid of Ariadne, its half-sister.

PERMESSUS (VI). A river descending from Mt Helicon in Boeotia, which was sacred to the Muses.

PHAETHON (VI). Phaethon was precocious enough to think himself capable of driving the fiery horses of his father, the Sun, and came to grief in the attempt. His sisters, who had abetted him in the adventure, mourned him so inconsolably that the gods in their pity turned them into trees (alders, here; in other versions, poplars).

PHILOMELA (VI). Philomela and Procne were daughters of Pandion, King of Athens. In the version of the story here followed by Virgil, Philomela was married to Tereus of Thrace and became the mother of Itylus. Tereus fell in love with his sister-in-law, Procne, violated her, and cut out her tongue to prevent her from denouncing him to his wife. She managed, however, to weave the information into a piece of cloth; and by way of revenge the sisters slew Itylus, served up his flesh to Tereus, and after the meal confronted him with his son's head. Then they fled, with Tereus in pursuit. All three were changed into birds, Tereus into a hoopoe, Procne into a swallow, and Philomela into a nightingale. In other versions of the tale, the names of the two ladies and of the birds they become are interchanged.

PHOEBUS APOLLO (III, IV, V, VI, VII, X). The son of Jove and Latona, and brother of Diana. He is the sun-god, and also the god of prophecy, of music and poetry, and of healing. In IV he is mentioned as the father of the poet Linus, and also in connexion with the return of the Golden Age. In V we see him as the shepherds' patron – he had himself been made to serve a man, Admetus, as a shepherd. In VI, as the god of inspiration, he advises Virgil on his poetic career. In the same Eclogue his choir, the Muses, acclaim the poet Gallus. And again, in X, he reappears to remonstrate with his lovelorn devotee.

PHYLLIS (III, V, VII, X). A country girl, mentioned in III as beloved by Iollas and Damoetas. In V she figures in the title of a song. In VII, the farmer Meliboeus deplores the fact that he has no such servant-girl to help him with the lambs. In the same poem Thyrsis and Corydon vie with each other in her praises. In X she is mentioned once more as a typical country beauty, whom Gallus would be glad to accept in exchange for his sophisticated actress friend.

PIERIAN (VI, VIII, X). Pieria was a district in the neighbourhood of Mt Olympus in Greece, connected from early times with the cult of the Muses, who are often referred to as Pierian goddesses.

PINDUS (X). A range of mountains in northern Greece. It was one of the traditional haunts of the Muses, whose functions the Naiads appear to be usurping in X, where Virgil disposes of their possible alibi on Pindus.

POLLIO (III, IV). Gaius Asinius Pollio, the poet, historian, and politician, and friend of Virgil. He was Consul in 40 B.C. (see Essay on IV) and played a leading part in the reconciliation of Octavian and Antony that was effected in that year and forms the background of Virgil's prophecy of a peaceful age. His poetry is mentioned in III and again in VIII, which appears to be dedicated to him. His works are lost.

PONTUS (VIII). A country in Asia Minor on the south coast of the Black Sea. It was the proverbial home of poisons and of poisoners.

PRIAPUS (VII). A minor deity, one of whose special functions was the protection of gardens.

PROETUS (VI). A king of Argos whose three daughters boasted that they were more beautiful than the goddess Here, and were punished by being made to imagine that they were cows. In the end they were cured of this delusion by the seer Melampus.

PROMETHEUS (VI). Originally a fire-god, Prometheus figures in Greek legend as the Titan who stole fire from heaven to give it to mankind, and was punished for his enterprise by Zeus. He was chained to a rock on Mt Caucasus, and his liver was pecked at by an eagle and perpetually renewed.

PYRRHA (VI). The wife of Deucalion, who, with her husband, is said to have created mankind, or created them afresh after the Flood, by throwing stones behind her back at the gods' command.

RHINE (X). Virgil dismisses the much-lauded river as typical of the back of beyond, and cold into the bargain. From the time of Julius Caesar it was the frontier river between Roman territory and the wilds of Germany.

RHODOPE (VI, VIII). A range of high mountains in Thrace, the country of the Orpheus legend.

ROME (I). The capital city of Italy. In I, its size and splendour are contrasted by a simple rustic visitor with the insignificance of his own market-town, the name of which is not given.

SARDINIAN (VII). The plant referred to is a kind of Ranunculus, the English celery-leaved crowfoot. Its bitterness is said to have given rise to the expression 'sardonic smile'.

SATURN (IV, VI). A god of agriculture in early Italian mythology. Later he was identified with the Greek Cronos, who was dethroned by his son Zeus. His name is connected with a time when the earth enjoyed a Golden Age.

SCYLLA (VI). There were two creatures of this name, whom Virgil and other Roman poets appear to have confused. The monster described here is obviously the Scylla whom Odysseus encountered on his travels

(*Odyssey*, XII); but this Scylla was the daughter of Phorcys and Cratais. Scylla the daughter of Nisus suffered a more complete but less revolting transformation and became a bird.

SCYTHIA (I). The wild and remote region which we know as southern Russia.

SIBYLLINE (IV). See Essay on IV.

SICILIAN (II, IV, VI, X). In the introductory lines of IV and VI Virgil uses the name by way of acknowledging his indebtedness to Theocritus, the pastoral poet who laid the scene of many of his Idyls in Sicily. In X the reference is to the story of Arethusa the Syracusan Nymph (see under *Arethusa*).

SILENUS (VI). See Essay on VI.

SILVANUS (X). An Italian woodland deity.

SOPHOCLES (VIII). The great Athenian dramatist (496–406 B.C.).

STIMICHON (V). A shepherd mentioned in V as an appreciative critic of music.

TEREUS (VI). See under *Philomela*.

THALIA (VI). The Muse of pastoral poetry and of comedy.

THESTYLIS (II). A country wench who is represented in II as waiting on the reapers.

THYRSIS (VII). The defeated contestant in the singing-match with Corydon, where they are described as 'Arcadians both'.

TIMAVUS (VIII). A river in north-eastern Italy, forming the boundary between Venetia and Istria.

TIPHYS (IV). The helmsman of the famous *Argo* in the expedition in search of the Golden Fleece.

TITYRUS (I, III, VI, VIII, IX). In I he is an elderly countryman who has saved his farm from seizure, and incidentally purchased his freedom, by a timely journey to Rome and application to the highest authorities. In III he is mentioned as a goatherd looking after

Damon's flocks. In VI his name is playfully used by Apollo in addressing Virgil himself as a pastoral poet – our only real justification for identifying Virgil with Tityrus. In VIII he is referred to as a typical shepherd-musician, and in IX is once more told to look after someone else's goats.

TMAROS (VIII). A mountain in Epirus.

VARIUS (IX). Lucius Varius Rufus, a distinguished poet of the Augustan age, who won the friendship of Virgil, Horace, and Maecenas. His works have not survived. See also Essay on IX.

VARUS (VI, IX). The Varus to whom Virgil addresses VI and whom he mentions in IX as the recipient of the poetical appeal on behalf of the Mantuan lands is usually identified with Publius Alfenus Varus. Servius tells us that this same Varus had studied philosophy with Virgil under Siro the Epicurean and that he was one of the commissioners appointed to allot lands to veterans in Northern Italy. The identification is doubtful.

VENUS (VII). The goddess of Love (Greek Aphrodite).

VESPER (VI). The evening or the evening star.